**Do brainteasers or computer games have
a positive impact on brain activity?**

*The answer is a resounding "yes." For the last fifteen years we have known
that the brain is elastic and it remains so until late in life. Its structure
develops constantly as a reaction to your experiences. The more your brain is
stimulated, the better your mental condition will be.*

An active brain is a better brain.

*Proverbial wisdom says "a healthy mind in a healthy body." So you are in
control of at least part of this equation. Tests have shown that physical
exertion stimulates neurogenesis: those who exercise make significantly
more brain cells, which are also granted a longer life. More brain cells ensure
better brainpower and better long-term memory.*

Brain sport at its best.

*This book offers a huge variety of puzzles that will exercise your brain. The
puzzles test logical insight, the ability to concentrate, and memory and
knowledge. Puzzle solving will not give you a super brain, but you will learn
skills for remembering things better and give certain brain activities an extra
boost. If you can't solve certain puzzles, don't look up the answers—just try
again later. Finding the solution is much more fun than knowing the solution.*

1. Word Search

Word searches are one of the most popular types of puzzles. The object of this puzzle is to find and mark all the hidden words inside the grid. The words may be hidden horizontally, vertically or diagonally, in both directions. The letters that remain unused form a key word when read in reading direction.

Hints:

An efficient method for finding the words is to go through the puzzle per column and look for the first letter of the word. If you find one, then look at the surrounding letters to see if the next letter is there. Do this until you find the whole word. Another useful strategy is to look for words with double letters or letters that are highly noticeable such as Q, X and Z.

2. Sudoku

The classic Sudoku with a 9x9 grid is still the most popular one. These completely irresistible, totally addictive puzzles offer a fun challenge that keeps fans entertained for hours. All of our Sudokus can be solved by using logic and were created using human logarithms. You should never have to guess what figure to use.

3. Anagrams

Rearrange the letters of a word or phrase to produce a new word or phrase, using all the original letters exactly once; for example "give her two" can be rearranged into "overweight". Extra letters are already in the right place.

4. Letter Blocks

Move the letter blocks around to form words on top and below that you can associate with a theme. In some puzzles, on one or two blocks, the letter from the top row has been switched with the letter from the bottom row.

5. Brainteasers

To solve our brainteasers you must think logically. Use one or several strategies such as direction, differences and/or similarities, associations, calculations, order, spatial insight, colors, quantities, and distances. Our brainteasers ensure that all of the brain's capacities are utilized.

6. Golf mazes

Start at the cell with a ball and a number on it. Then draw the shortest route from the ball to the hole, the only square without a number. You can only move along vertical and horizontal lines, but not along diagonals. The figure on each square indicates the number of squares the ball must move in the same direction. You can change directions at each stop.

Hints:
Start at the hole and try to find the cell from where you can reach the hole, and then start from the ball.

7. One Letter Less or More
The word below contains the letters of the word above plus or minus the letter in the middle. One letter is already in the right place.

8. Binairo®

1	0	1	0	1	0	0	1	1	0
0	1	0	0	1	1	0	0	1	1
0	0	1	1	0	1	1	0	0	1
1	0	0	1	1	0	0	1	1	0
0	1	1	0	0	1	1	0	0	1
1	0	0	1	0	1	1	0	1	0
0	1	1	0	1	0	0	1	0	1
0	0	1	0	0	1	1	0	1	1
1	1	0	1	0	0	1	1	0	0
1	1	0	1	1	0	0	1	0	0

Hey, puzzle fans, get ready for a great new number challenge: Binairo®. These puzzles are just as simple and challenging as Sudoku, but that is where the similarity ends.

Just fill in the grid until there are five zeros and five ones in every row and every column. You can't have more than two of the same number next to or under each other, or have two identical rows or columns.

Hints:
Look for duos of the same number and put the other number before and behind it. Try to avoid trios by entering a zero between two ones or a one between two zeros. Don't

forget to count: if you already have five zeros in a row or column, fill in the rest with ones.

9. Word Pyramid
Each word in the pyramid has the letters of the word above it, plus a new letter.

Hints:
Work your way down from top to bottom. If you can't solve a word, skip the line and try to solve the next one.

10. Doodle puzzle
A doodle puzzle is a combination of images, letters and/or numbers that indicate a word or a concept.

Hints:
If you cannot solve a doodle puzzle, do not look at the answer right away but come back later. Try to think outside the box.

11. Find the Word

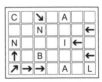

Knowing that every arrow points to a letter and that no letter can touch another vertically, horizontally or diagonally, find the missing letters that form a key word when read in order. We show one letter in a circle to help you get started.

Hints:
Cross out all letters that are surrounding a letter that you have found.

12. Connect

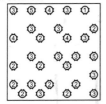 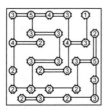

Link all circles with straight horizontal or vertical lines into one connected group. The numbers tell how many lines are connected to a circle. There can be no more than two lines in the same direction and lines cannot cross circles or other lines.

Hints:
A one cannot connect to another one. A two cannot have two connections to another two. A three in a corner must have at least one connection in each direction. A four in a corner has two connections in each direction. A five at the edge must have at least one connection in each direction. A six at the edge has two connections in each direction. A seven in the middle must have at least one connection in each direction. An eight in the middle has two connections in each direction.

So your challenge is to give your brain the best workout it can have, and every one of these puzzles will do that. Enjoy the challenge.

Word Search

MEDIUM NEW YORK

BIG APPLE
BRONX
CINEMA
DUTCH
GERSHWIN
GIULIANI
HUDSON
IRISH
KNICKS
METS
NASDAQ
OPERA
PACINO
TENNIS

N	A	S	D	A	Q	N	N	S
O	E	L	P	P	A	G	I	B
S	T	E	M	O	X	N	W	E
D	S	O	W	P	N	H	H	C
U	K	N	Y	E	O	S	S	I
H	C	I	T	R	R	I	R	N
O	I	C	R	A	B	R	E	E
I	N	A	I	L	U	I	G	M
K	K	P	H	C	T	U	D	A

*All the words are hidden vertically, horizontally,
or diagonally, in both directions. The letters that remain
unused form a key word when read in order.*

MEDIUM

6	3	7					1	4
1	5	8	4					2
4	9	2		7				
5	4	3	2					
2	8	1			4		5	8
7	6	9						1
		4	6		3	8	9	
3		5			7			6
		6		2	8		3	5

*Fill in the grid so that each row, each column,
and each 3x3 frame contains every number from 1 to 9.*

MEDIUM

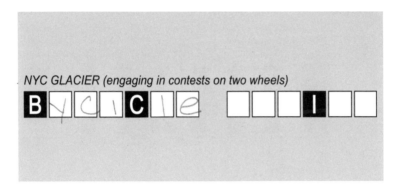

NYC GLACIER (engaging in contests on two wheels)

B Y C I C l e ☐ ☐ ☐ I ☐ ☐

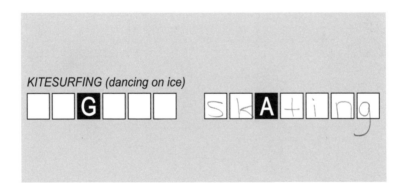

KITESURFING (dancing on ice)

☐ ☐ G ☐ ☐ ☐ S K A t i n g

Form the word or phrase that is described in parentheses with the letters above the grid. Extra letters are already in the right place.

MEDIUM

S	G	I	N	T	O	N
T	K	O	H	W	E	R

Solution

Move the letter blocks around to form words on top
and below that you can associate with **internet**.
The letters are reversed on one block.

HARD

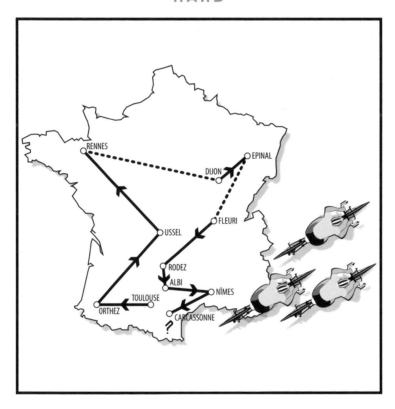

What is the first letter of the city where the cyclists that departed from Carcassonne will arrive?

MEDIUM

0	3	3	3	1	4
(1)	4	3	2	1	4
1	2	3	1	2	4
1	2	1	0	1	○
1	3	1	4	2	2
3	5	3	1	2	3

Draw the shortest path from the ball to the hole. You can only move along vertical and horizontal lines. The figure on each square indicates the number of squares the ball must move in the same direction. You can change direction at each stop.

HARD

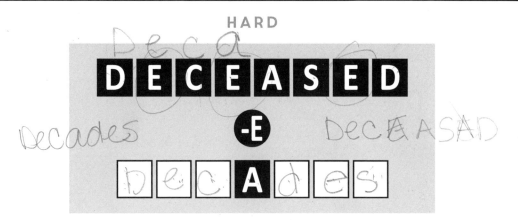

The word below contains the letters of the word above plus or minus the letter in the middle. One letter is already in the right place.

MEDIUM

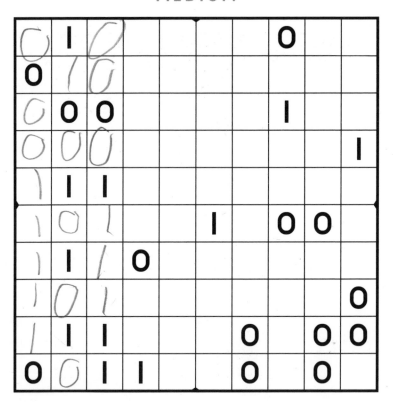

Complete the grid with zeros and ones until there are five zeros and five ones in every row and every column. No more than two of the same number can be next to or under each other. Rows or columns with exactly the same content are not allowed.

MEDIUM

(1) exists

(2) man

(3) danger

(4) worn by women

(5) tricycles

(6) hits

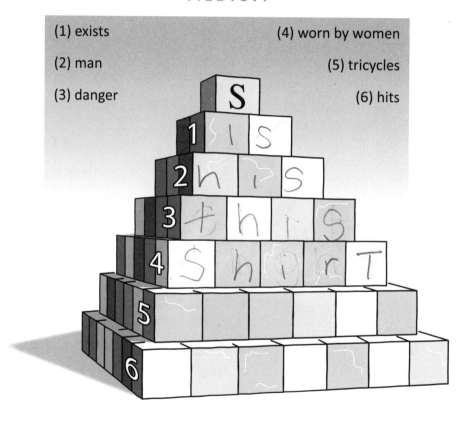

*Each word in the pyramid has the letters of
the word above it, plus a new letter.*

MEDIUM

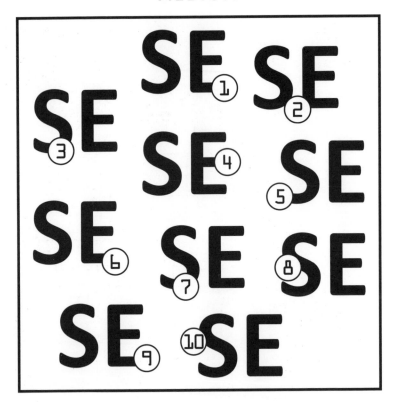

*What word or concept
is depicted here?*

Find The Word

MEDIUM

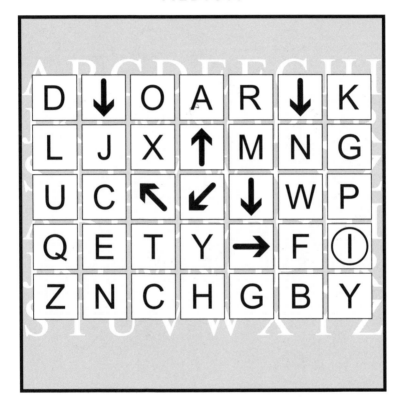

D	↓	O	A	R	↓	K
L	J	X	↑	M	N	G
U	C	↖	↙	↓	W	P
Q	E	T	Y	→	F	Ⓘ
Z	N	C	H	G	B	Y

Knowing that every arrow points to a letter and that no letter can touch another vertically, horizontally, or diagonally, find the missing letters that form a key word when read in order. We show one letter in a circle to help you get started.

MEDIUM

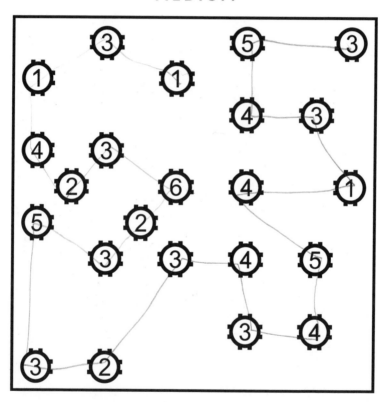

*Link all circles with straight horizontal or vertical lines into
one connected group. The numbers tell how many lines are
connected to a circle. There can be no more than two lines in
the same direction and lines cannot cross circles or other lines.*

Word Search

BENCH
COMPOST
DROUGHT
GREEN
HUMUS
LAWN
MOLD
NETTLE
POND
PRUNE
RAKE
SAND
TEMPERATE
WATERFALL

T	H	G	U	O	R	D	G	H
L	C	E	P	R	U	N	E	U
A	N	K	D	M	O	L	D	M
W	E	A	N	E	E	R	G	U
N	B	R	O	S	A	N	D	S
T	E	M	P	E	R	A	T	E
N	E	T	T	L	E	A	R	D
L	L	A	F	R	E	T	A	W
E	C	O	M	P	O	S	T	N

*All the words are hidden vertically, horizontally,
or diagonally, in both directions. The letters that remain
unused form a key word when read in order.*

HARD

		8		1				
		4		8	9			
			7	9		8		
	2					7		
		9					6	2
	9		6				8	
	5		1	2				3
3		2					4	7

*Fill in the grid so that each row, each column,
and each 3x3 frame contains every number from 1 to 9.*

Anagrams

A DAYDREAM (Merit for performance in motion picture)

| | C | A | | | | | | W | | | |

TERRY SLEEP (Oscar Best Actress 2012)

| M | | | | | | | | | | |

Form the word or phrase that is described in parentheses with the letters above the grid. Extra letters are already in the right place.

HARD

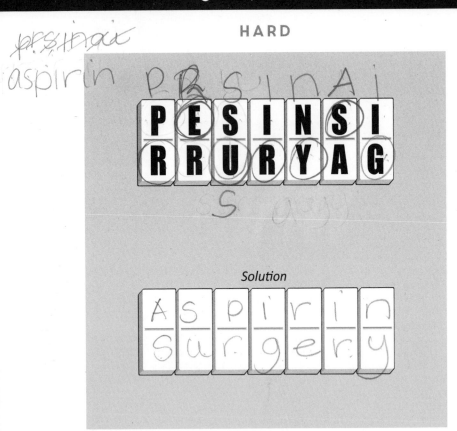

Solution

*Move the letter blocks around to form words on top
and below that you can associate with **healthcare**.
The letters are reversed on two blocks.*

VERY HARD

Which pattern (1-6) should replace the question mark?

Golf Maze

3	5	5	5	1	2
2	2	3	1	2	3	4
3	2	1	3	3	2
5	4	2	3	3	5
2	1	4	1	2	●
2	2	1	5	1	2

Draw the shortest path from the ball to the hole. You can only move along vertical and horizontal lines. The figure on each square indicates the number of squares the ball must move in the same direction. You can change direction at each stop.

HARD

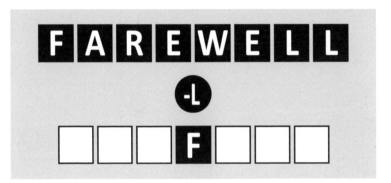

FAREWELL

-L

☐ ☐ ☐ **F** ☐ ☐ ☐

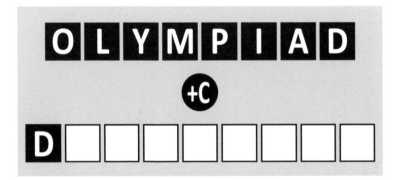

OLYMPIAD

+C

D ☐ ☐ ☐ ☐ ☐ ☐ ☐ ☐

The word below contains the letters of the word above plus or minus the letter in the middle. One letter is already in the right place.

HARD

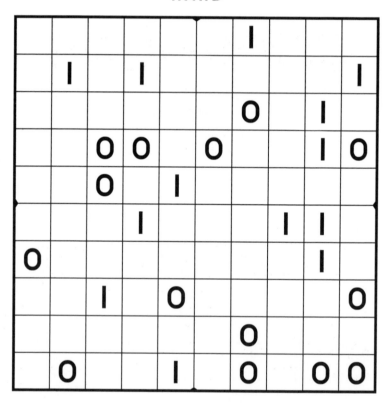

Complete the grid with zeros and ones until there are five zeros and five ones in every row and every column. No more than two of the same number can be next to or under each other. Rows or columns with exactly the same content are not allowed.

Word Pyramid

MEDIUM

(1) in the direction of

(2) large amount

(3) unable to be found

(4) took secretly

(5) inexpensive lodging place for travelers

(6) leather case for a pistol

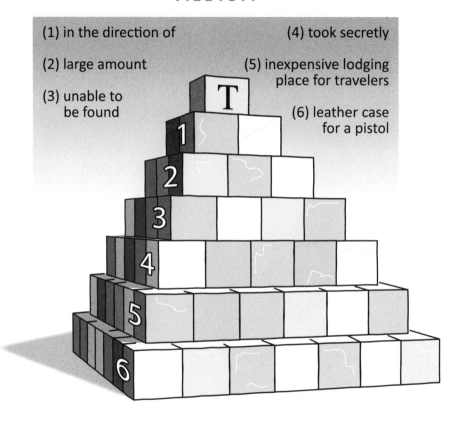

Each word in the pyramid has the letters of the word above it, plus a new letter.

MEDIUM

*What word or concept
is depicted here?*

Find The Word

HARD

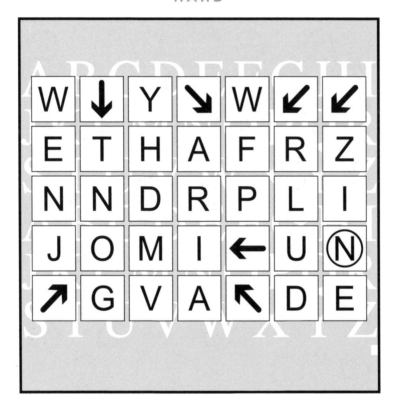

Knowing that every arrow points to a letter and that no letter can touch another vertically, horizontally, or diagonally, find the missing letters that form a key word when read in order. We show one letter in a circle to help you get started.

HARD

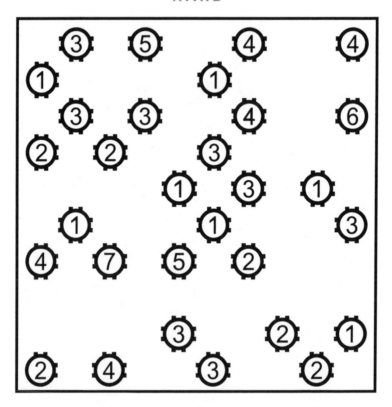

Link all circles with straight horizontal or vertical lines into one connected group. The numbers tell how many lines are connected to a circle. There can be no more than two lines in the same direction and lines cannot cross circles or other lines.

Word Search

CHEAP
COLA
DORITOS
EXTRA
FATTY
GYROS
HOT DOG
KEBAB
KETCHUP
NUTS
OBESITY
OVEN
PIZZA
SNACKS
SUGAR

O	B	E	S	I	T	Y	E	C
G	O	D	T	O	H	X	O	B
R	A	G	U	S	T	L	A	D
F	Z	Y	S	R	A	B	A	O
F	Z	R	A	N	E	P	V	R
A	I	O	S	K	A	E	T	I
T	P	S	F	E	N	C	O	T
T	P	U	H	C	T	E	K	O
Y	O	C	N	U	T	S	D	S

*All the words are hidden vertically, horizontally,
or diagonally, in both directions. The letters that remain
unused form a key word when read in order.*

Sudoku

9	2		1	5	8			4
		8		9				5
		1						
6			5	8		1		
		4	3		2			
	4	2				8	3	
1			6			7	4	

Fill in the grid so that each row, each column,
and each 3x3 frame contains every number from 1 to 9.

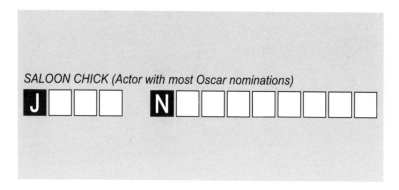

SALOON CHICK *(Actor with most Oscar nominations)*

J □ □ □   N □ □ □ □ □ □ □ □

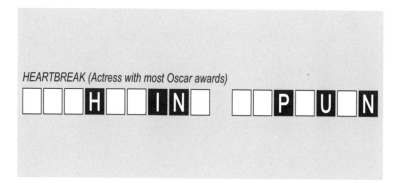

HEARTBREAK *(Actress with most Oscar awards)*

□ □ □ H □ IN □   □ □ P □ U □ N

Form the word or phrase that is described in parentheses with the letters above the grid. Extra letters are already in the right place.

EASY

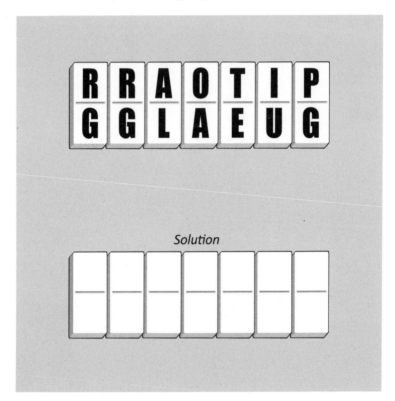

R	R	A	O	T	I	P
G	G	L	A	E	U	G

Solution

*Move the letter blocks around to form words on top
and below that you can associate with **travel**.*

HARD

How many people are in one skiff?

MEDIUM

4	4	4	5	2	4
1	1	4	1	0	1
5	4	1	2	1	4
1	1	1	3	1	2
2	2	4	2	3	3
1	2	1	4		1

Draw the shortest path from the ball to the hole. You can only move along vertical and horizontal lines. The figure on each square indicates the number of squares the ball must move in the same direction. You can change direction at each stop.

HARD

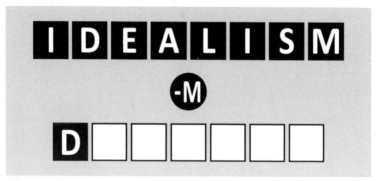

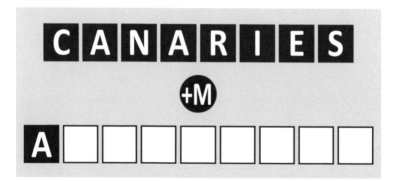

*The word below contains the letters of the word
above plus or minus the letter in the middle.
One letter is already in the right place.*

EASY

				0		I		0	
0									
		0				I		I	
			I		0			I	
			I				0		
		0							I
						0			
		I		I				I	
0		I					I	I	
				I		I			

Complete the grid with zeros and ones until there are five zeros and five ones in every row and every column. No more than two of the same number can be next to or under each other. Rows or columns with exactly the same content are not allowed.

Word Pyramid

(1) in the Christian era

(2) boy

(3) placed

(4) perfect

(5) dames

(6) misdirect

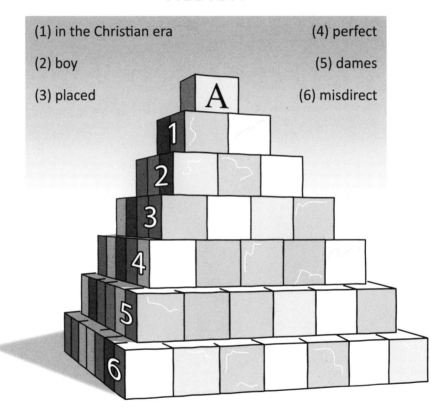

*Each word in the pyramid has the letters of
the word above it, plus a new letter.*

MEDIUM

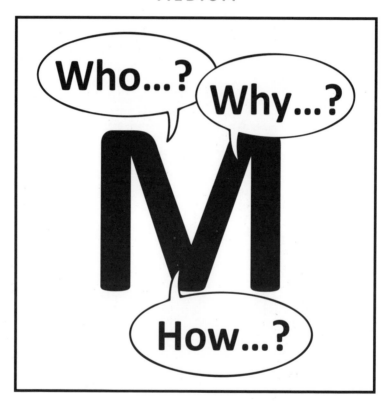

*What word or concept
is depicted here?*

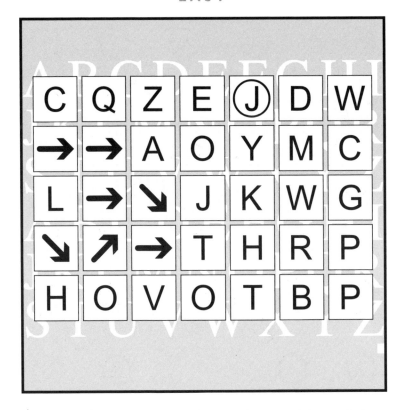

Find The Word

EASY

C	Q	Z	E	Ⓙ	D	W
→	→	A	O	Y	M	C
L	→	↘	J	K	W	G
↘	↗	→	T	H	R	P
H	O	V	O	T	B	P

Knowing that every arrow points to a letter and that no letter can touch another vertically, horizontally, or diagonally, find the missing letters that form a key word when read in order. We show one letter in a circle to help you get started.

EASY

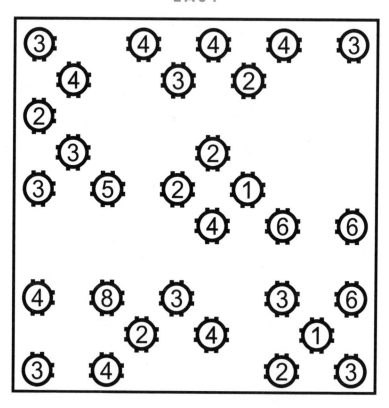

Link all circles with straight horizontal or vertical lines into
one connected group. The numbers tell how many lines are
connected to a circle. There can be no more than two lines in
the same direction and lines cannot cross circles or other lines.

Word Search

ALCATRAZ
BEACHES
BEAR
DESERT
ENGLISH
FORESTS
GETTY
GOLD
HILLS
LAKES
REDWOOD
SMOG
UCLA
WARNER

E	N	G	L	I	S	H	Z	C
B	E	A	C	H	E	S	A	R
D	D	O	O	W	D	E	R	E
D	E	U	A	H	L	K	T	N
L	G	S	C	I	I	A	A	R
O	F	O	E	L	B	L	C	A
G	O	R	M	R	A	E	L	W
F	O	R	E	S	T	S	A	S
N	I	G	E	T	T	Y	A	R

All the words are hidden vertically, horizontally, or diagonally, in both directions. The letters that remain unused form a key word when read in order.

EASY

5			9	6				1
			2		3	9		
	9				1	3	5	6
1	5		8		7	4		
3	4		1					
6	2	8	4	3		1	7	
		2	5				1	
		6						7

*Fill in the grid so that each row, each column,
and each 3x3 frame contains every number from 1 to 9.*

MEDIUM

GIANT SHOW *(The Evergreen State)*

					N				

MISS RIO *(The Show-Me State)*

				U		

Form the word or phrase that is described in parentheses with the letters above the grid. Extra letters are already in the right place.

Letter Blocks

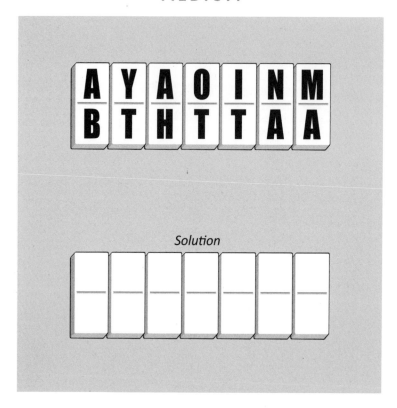

Solution

*Move the letter blocks around to form words on top and below that you can associate with **biology**. The letters are reversed on one block.*

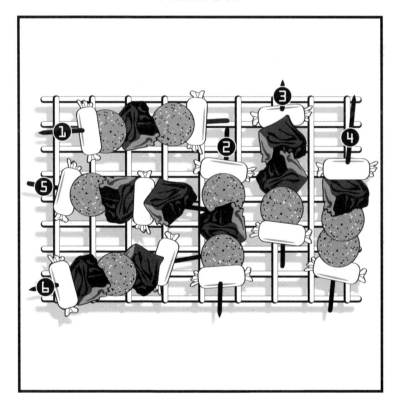

Which kebab (1-6) does not belong?

Golf Maze

MEDIUM

4	2	4	4	2	3
1	1	4	1	2	
4	4	1	3	1	4
4	3	1	2	1	5
1	1	4	4	2	2
3	3	5	4	1	4

Draw the shortest path from the ball to the hole. You can only move along vertical and horizontal lines. The figure on each square indicates the number of squares the ball must move in the same direction. You can change direction at each stop.

HARD

HANDLING

-H

L ☐ ☐ ☐ ☐ ☐ ☐

REACTION

+N

☐ ☐ ☐ **T** ☐ ☐ ☐ ☐ ☐

The word below contains the letters of the word above plus or minus the letter in the middle. One letter is already in the right place.

Binairo®

MEDIUM

I						O	I		
					O				I
			I					I	I
			I						
		O				I		O	
				O				O	O
			O	O					
O									
					I	I		I	I
					I			O	

Complete the grid with zeros and ones until there are five zeros and five ones in every row and every column. No more than two of the same number can be next to or under each other. Rows or columns with exactly the same content are not allowed.

Word Pyramid

MEDIUM

(1) medical practitioner

(2) crazy

(3) produced

(4) mass communication

(5) look up to

(6) half fish

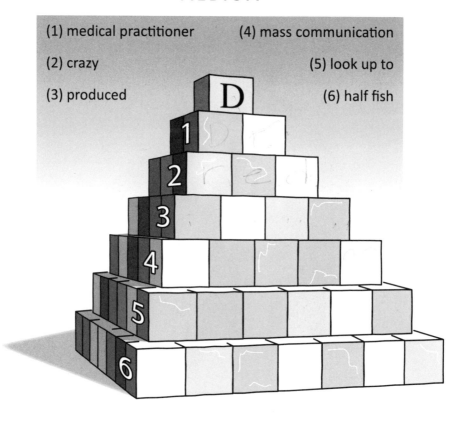

*Each word in the pyramid has the letters of
the word above it, plus a new letter.*

MEDIUM

*What word or concept
is depicted here?*

Find The Word

MEDIUM

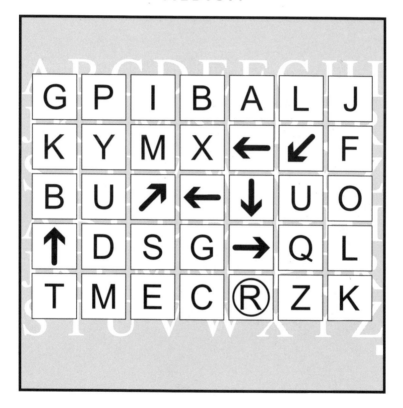

G	P	I	B	A	L	J
K	Y	M	X	←	↙	F
B	U	↗	←	↓	U	O
↑	D	S	G	→	Q	L
T	M	E	C	Ⓡ	Z	K

Knowing that every arrow points to a letter and that no letter can touch another vertically, horizontally, or diagonally, find the missing letters that form a key word when read in order. We show one letter in a circle to help you get started.

Connect

MEDIUM

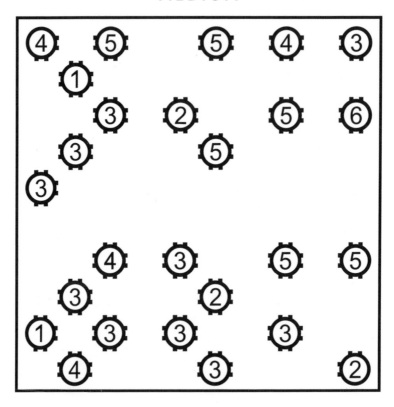

Link all circles with straight horizontal or vertical lines into one connected group. The numbers tell how many lines are connected to a circle. There can be no more than two lines in the same direction and lines cannot cross circles or other lines.

MEDIUM

BUILD
CLIMB
COUNT
CYCLE
HORMONES
INFANT
LEARN
MOVE
MUSIC
PARENTS
SKILLS
SOCIAL
SWIM
TODDLER
WRITE

P	A	R	E	N	T	S	C	H
I	L	M	I	W	S	I	S	H
C	N	C	O	U	N	T	O	O
M	L	R	B	F	S	O	C	R
U	D	I	A	U	K	D	I	M
S	R	N	M	E	I	D	A	O
I	T	O	E	B	L	L	L	N
C	V	C	Y	C	L	E	D	E
E	T	I	R	W	S	R	N	S

All the words are hidden vertically, horizontally, or diagonally, in both directions. The letters that remain unused form a key word when read in order.

MEDIUM

	5	4	3		9	6		
7	9				2		4	1
1	3		6		4		9	
		7				8		
			9					
9	2		8	4			5	
6	7			9	8			
8					6	7		

*Fill in the grid so that each row, each column,
and each 3x3 frame contains every number from 1 to 9.*

Anagrams

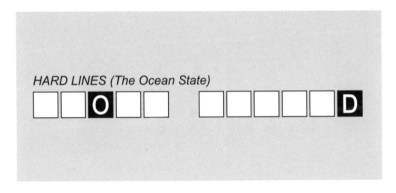

HARD LINES *(The Ocean State)*

| | | O | | | | | | | | D |

LEADER *(The First State)*

| | | | A | W | | | |

Form the word or phrase that is described in parentheses with the letters above the grid. Extra letters are already in the right place.

HARD

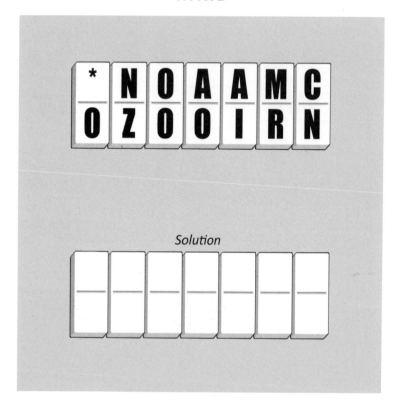

*Move the letter blocks around to form words on top and below that you can associate with **river**. The letters are reversed on two blocks.*

VERY HARD

NEWPORT
EVERSOR
VOVINO
ORLEMAN
RIMIN?

Which letter is missing in the name of the last port that the yachtsman will enter at the end of his voyage?

Golf Maze

MEDIUM

5	5	5	1	1	5
2	1	3	4	2	1
4	2	1	0	2	4
1	3	1	1	2	3
4	1	4	2	3	2
1	1	5		2	3

Draw the shortest path from the ball to the hole. You can only move along vertical and horizontal lines. The figure on each square indicates the number of squares the ball must move in the same direction. You can change direction at each stop.

HARD

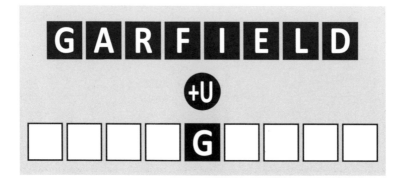

The word below contains the letters of the word above plus or minus the letter in the middle. One letter is already in the right place.

HARD

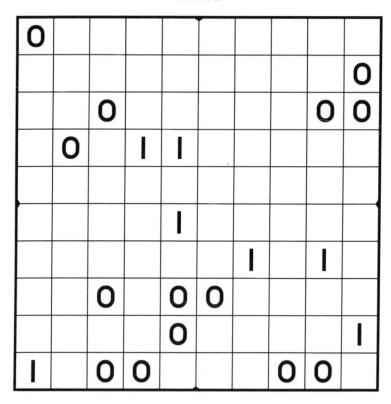

Complete the grid with zeros and ones until there are five zeros and five ones in every row and every column. No more than two of the same number can be next to or under each other. Rows or columns with exactly the same content are not allowed.

Word Pyramid

MEDIUM

(1) prefix for again

(2) organ

(3) beloved

(4) class

(5) risk

(6) interpreting something that is written

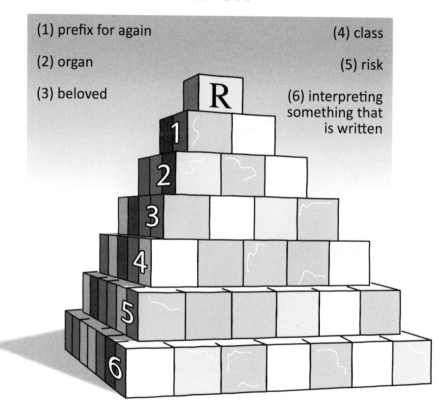

Each word in the pyramid has the letters of the word above it, plus a new letter.

HARD

*What word or concept
is depicted here?*

HARD

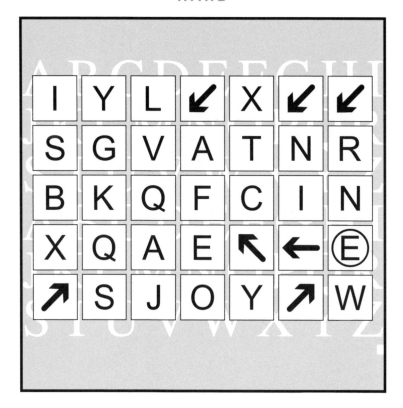

Knowing that every arrow points to a letter and that no letter can touch another vertically, horizontally, or diagonally, find the missing letters that form a key word when read in order. We show one letter in a circle to help you get started.

Connect

HARD

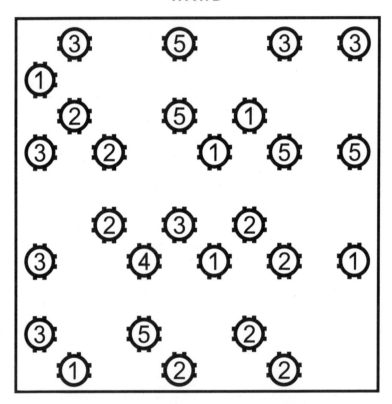

Link all circles with straight horizontal or vertical lines into one connected group. The numbers tell how many lines are connected to a circle. There can be no more than two lines in the same direction and lines cannot cross circles or other lines.

MEDIUM

ACTOR
AMATEUR
CHOIR
DRAMA
EPIC
GREEK
MAKE-UP
OPERA
PLAYHOUSE
REHEARSAL
SCENARIO
STUDIO
TRAGEDY
WINGS

P	O	P	E	R	A	L	T	H
L	E	R	U	E	T	A	M	A
A	G	R	E	E	K	S	D	R
Y	A	T	R	E	K	R	R	I
H	W	R	O	T	C	A	A	O
O	I	D	U	T	S	E	M	H
U	N	E	P	I	C	H	A	C
S	G	T	R	A	G	E	D	Y
E	S	C	E	N	A	R	I	O

*All the words are hidden vertically, horizontally,
or diagonally, in both directions. The letters that remain
unused form a key word when read in order.*

Sudoku

HARD

	4							
			6					
			9		1		7	
	7	5			2		6	3
8		4	7					2
	2					3		
9				7		4		
			1	3	6		8	

*Fill in the grid so that each row, each column,
and each 3x3 frame contains every number from 1 to 9.*

MEDIUM

DOGY RUN *(fastest dog)*

		E		H			

BEE WALL *(largest living mammal on earth)*

		U			H		

Form the word or phrase that is described in parentheses with the letters above the grid. Extra letters are already in the right place.

EASY

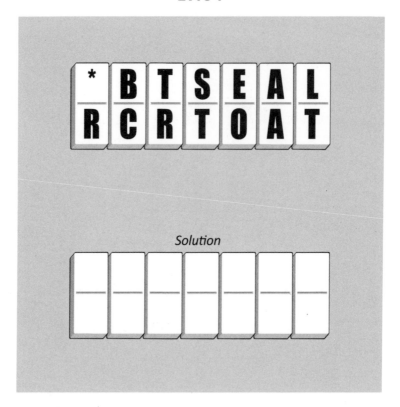

Solution

*Move the letter blocks around to form words on top
and below that you can associate with **agriculture**.*

MEDIUM

Which number is missing on the last face?

Golf Maze

MEDIUM

0	5	2	1	4	2
5	1	4	1	2	1
2	3	3	3	2	3
5	1	2	0	1	1
	2	3	1	1	2
5	1	2	2	1	2

Draw the shortest path from the ball to the hole. You can only move along vertical and horizontal lines. The figure on each square indicates the number of squares the ball must move in the same direction. You can change direction at each stop.

HARD

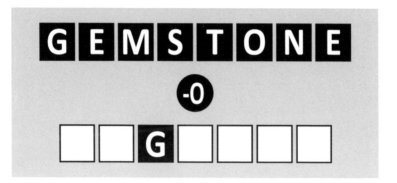

GEMSTONE

-O

[ ] [ ] [G] [ ] [ ] [ ] [ ]

MADHOUSE

+I

[ ] [ ] [U] [ ] [ ] [ ] [ ] [ ]

The word below contains the letters of the word above plus or minus the letter in the middle. One letter is already in the right place.

EASY

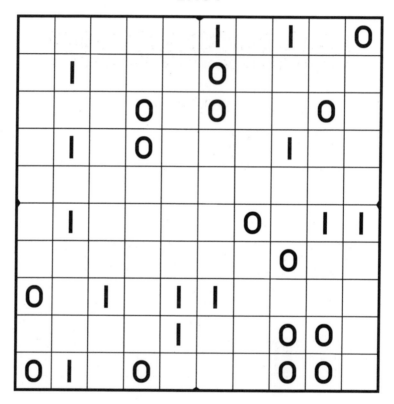

Complete the grid with zeros and ones until there are five zeros
and five ones in every row and every column. No more than two
of the same number can be next to or under each other. Rows
or columns with exactly the same content are not allowed.

MEDIUM

(1) exist

(2) unit of sound intensity equal to 10 decibels

(3) capable

(4) piece of furniture

(5) horse barn

(6) conflicts

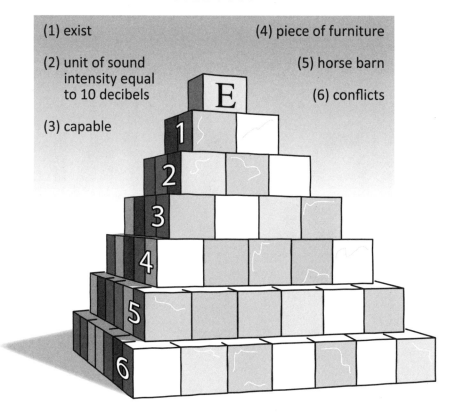

Each word in the pyramid has the letters of the word above it, plus a new letter.

MEDIUM

DOWN

What word or concept
is depicted here?

EASY

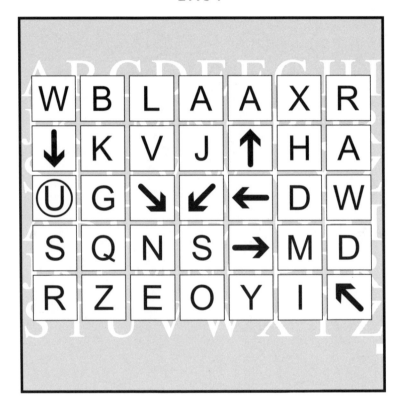

Knowing that every arrow points to a letter and that no letter can touch another vertically, horizontally, or diagonally, find the missing letters that form a key word when read in order. We show one letter in a circle to help you get started.

EASY

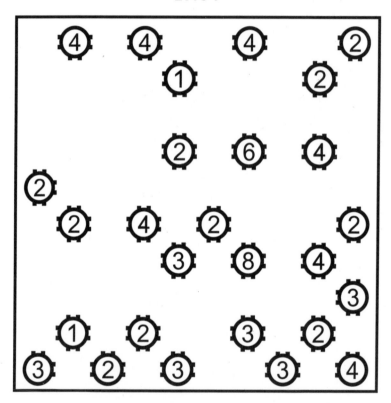

Link all circles with straight horizontal or vertical lines into
one connected group. The numbers tell how many lines are
connected to a circle. There can be no more than two lines in
the same direction and lines cannot cross circles or other lines.

MEDIUM

ANKLE
GLANDS
JAW
KNEE
LIGAMENT
LIVER
MEMBRANE
MOLAR
NERVE
ORGAN
PALATE
SCALP
TAIL BONE
THROAT
TONSILS

T	A	O	R	H	T	A	T	L
T	W	N	A	G	R	O	M	I
A	P	A	N	K	N	E	E	G
I	L	P	J	S	M	R	L	A
L	A	A	I	B	A	A	I	M
B	C	L	R	A	N	L	V	E
O	S	A	T	D	K	O	E	N
N	N	T	S	O	L	M	R	T
E	M	E	Y	N	E	R	V	E

All the words are hidden vertically, horizontally, or diagonally, in both directions. The letters that remain unused form a key word when read in order.

VERY HARD

8				7	2			1
3						6		4
	2	6			3			
	1		5			2	3	
		9	1		7			
				4			9	
						5	8	2
	3							
	4							

*Fill in the grid so that each row, each column,
and each 3x3 frame contains every number from 1 to 9.*

MEDIUM

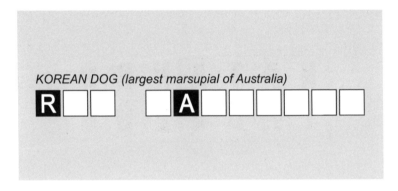

KOREAN DOG *(largest marsupial of Australia)*

| R | | | | A | | | | | |

GINGER ALE *(largest big cat in India)*

| B | | | | | | T | | | |

Form the word or phrase that is described in parentheses with the letters above the grid. Extra letters are already in the right place.

MEDIUM

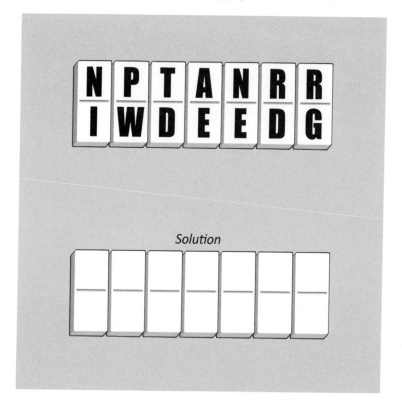

Solution

Move the letter blocks around to form words on top
and below that you can associate with **marriage**.
The letters are reversed on one block.

HARD

Which piece (1-6) completes the cube?

MEDIUM

3	2	1	4	1	2
3	2	4	1	2	2
2	2	2	1	4	
3	2	2	3	1	5
3	4	4	2	2	5
3	1	5	1	5	0

Draw the shortest path from the ball to the hole. You can only move along vertical and horizontal lines. The figure on each square indicates the number of squares the ball must move in the same direction. You can change direction at each stop.

HARD

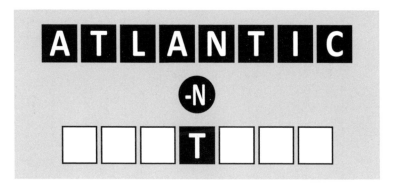

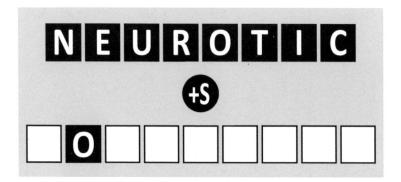

The word below contains the letters of the word above plus or minus the letter in the middle. One letter is already in the right place.

Binairo®

MEDIUM

				I				O
	O		O		O			
						I		I
		I	I				I	
		I		O		O		O	O
								O	
I		O		I		O	O		
									I
I	O		I	I			O		I

Complete the grid with zeros and ones until there are five zeros and five ones in every row and every column. No more than two of the same number can be next to or under each other. Rows or columns with exactly the same content are not allowed.

Word Pyramid

MEDIUM

(1) note

(2) from a great distance

(3) flat float

(4) later

(5) parent

(6) plume

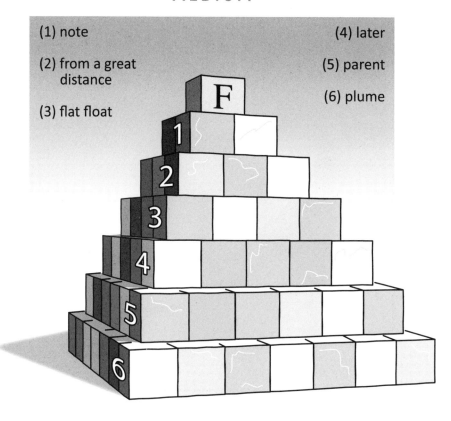

Each word in the pyramid has the letters of the word above it, plus a new letter.

MEDIUM

*What word or concept
is depicted here?*

MEDIUM

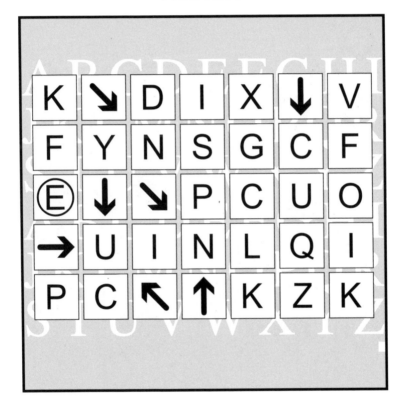

Knowing that every arrow points to a letter and that no letter can touch another vertically, horizontally, or diagonally, find the missing letters that form a key word when read in order. We show one letter in a circle to help you get started.

Connect

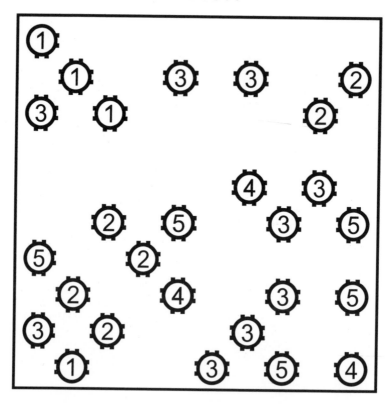

Link all circles with straight horizontal or vertical lines into
one connected group. The numbers tell how many lines are
connected to a circle. There can be no more than two lines in
the same direction and lines cannot cross circles or other lines.

MEDIUM

AMOROUS
BLUE
CHANGE
CUBISM
DRINK
ETCHINGS
EVA
LOLA
MUSEUM
OLGA
PALOMA
ROSE
RUIZ
SCULPTOR
STUDIO

O	P	C	H	A	N	G	E	I
L	O	I	D	U	T	S	T	C
G	R	O	T	P	L	U	C	S
A	M	S	I	B	U	C	H	U
A	L	D	R	I	N	K	I	O
A	M	O	L	A	P	R	N	R
A	S	B	L	U	E	U	G	O
S	V	R	O	S	E	I	S	M
M	U	E	S	U	M	Z	O	A

*All the words are hidden vertically, horizontally,
or diagonally, in both directions. The letters that remain
unused form a key word when read in order.*

EASY

			1					
			8		6			7
	1						4	
9		8						
		7		6		8		
		1	4		8	9	7	5
1	7	6	5		2			9
5				3				4
3		2	9		1		5	

*Fill in the grid so that each row, each column,
and each 3x3 frame contains every number from 1 to 9.*

MEDIUM

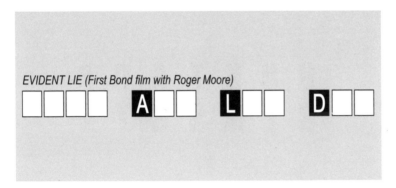

EVIDENT LIE (First Bond film with Roger Moore)

☐☐☐☐ **A**☐☐ **L**☐☐ **D**☐☐

THIN TOMATO (Played Bond in 'Licence to Kill')

☐☐☐☐☐☐**Y** **D**☐**L**☐☐☐

Form the word or phrase that is described in parentheses with the letters above the grid. Extra letters are already in the right place.

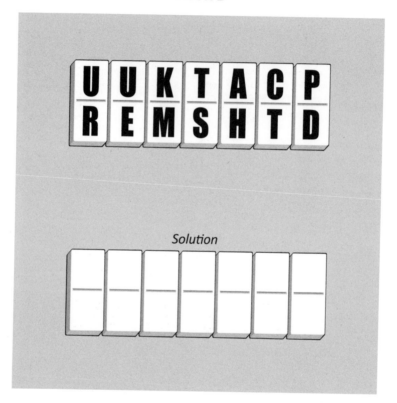

Letter Blocks

HARD

Solution

Move the letter blocks around to form words on top
and below that you can associate with **sauces**.
The letters are reversed on two blocks.

MEDIUM

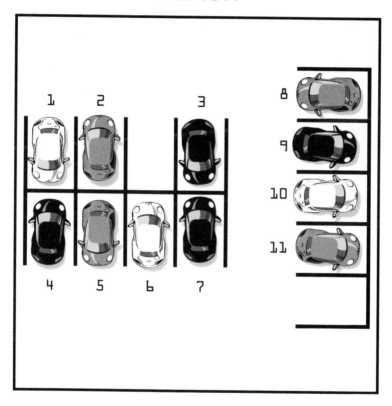

Which car (1-11) is parked incorrectly?

MEDIUM

5	1	5	4	4	1
5	1	1	4	4	2
1	3	3	3	3	4
5	4	3		1	5
3	2	4	3	1	5
2	1	2	5	4	4

Draw the shortest path from the ball to the hole. You can only move along vertical and horizontal lines. The figure on each square indicates the number of squares the ball must move in the same direction. You can change direction at each stop.

HARD

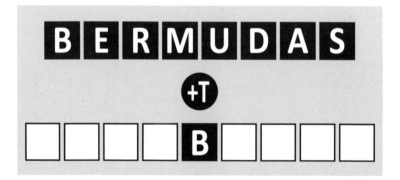

The word below contains the letters of the word above plus or minus the letter in the middle. One letter is already in the right place.

HARD

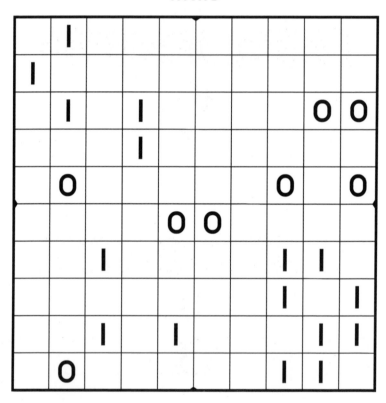

Complete the grid with zeros and ones until there are five zeros and five ones in every row and every column. No more than two of the same number can be next to or under each other. Rows or columns with exactly the same content are not allowed.

Word Pyramid

(1) the thing

(2) be seated

(3) spatter

(4) dismantle

(5) clergyman

(6) buccaneers

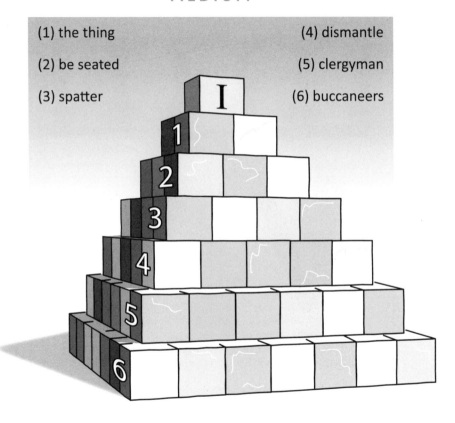

Each word in the pyramid has the letters of the word above it, plus a new letter.

MEDIUM

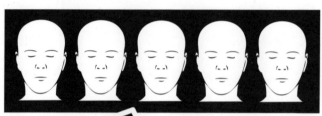

Lorem ipsum dolor si... ec-
tetuer adipiscir ... it
facilisis nibh. C .uit
lacus. Vivamus eu odi ... .a.
eros. Praesent urna r ... enei ...
vel, egestas et, tem ... , odio. Sed
tincidunt, elit ve' ... .is egestas,
nisi ante fringil' ... n, id aliquet
enim sapien s ... quam. Donec
vitae diam a ... oreet pulvinar.
Sed euismoc ... .c pede.
Curabitur c ... .iisi. Donec pulvinar condimentum tellus. Vivamus
varius. Duis viverra, velit vel venena-
tis ultricies, magna felis commodo
mi, non mollis est nulla a ipsum.

Donec et felis sed justo adipiscing
lacinia. In hac habitasse platea dic-
tumst. Fusce dui.
Pellentesque habitant morbi tristi-
que senectus et netus et malesuada
fames ac turpis egestas. Nulla a
augue quis ante viverra porta. Class
aptent taciti sociosqu ad litora
torquent per conubia nostra, per
inceptos himenaeos. Suspendisse
justo turpis, faucibus ac, volutpat
dignissim, elementum nec, nisi.
Etiam pede ante, tincidunt ac, porta
ac, blandit vel, lectus. Lorem ipsum
dolor sit amet, consectetuer adipiscing elit. In suscipit facilisis nibh.

*What word or concept
is depicted here?*

Find The Word

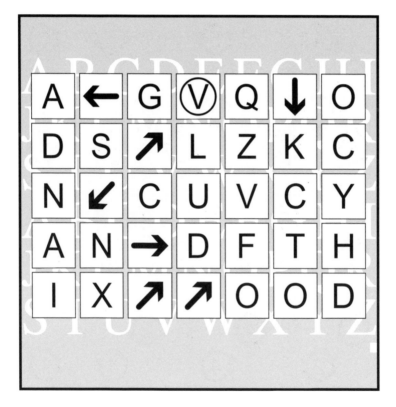

Knowing that every arrow points to a letter and that no letter can touch another vertically, horizontally, or diagonally, find the missing letters that form a key word when read in order. We show one letter in a circle to help you get started.

HARD

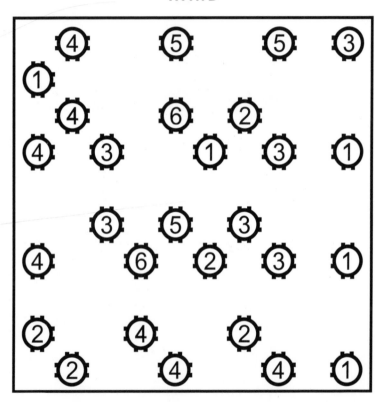

Link all circles with straight horizontal or vertical lines into one connected group. The numbers tell how many lines are connected to a circle. There can be no more than two lines in the same direction and lines cannot cross circles or other lines.

Word Search

ALIEN
AURA
BIRDS
BLACK
CARRIE
CHRISTINE
DEMON
GHOST
GREMLINS
HANNIBAL
HYDE
JAWS
OMEN
SATAN
VOODOO

```
H H O R J A W S E
A B L A C K C N N
N R N E I L A I I
N D E M O N R L T
I A M E S S R M S
B R O A D O I E I
A U T R R Y E R R
L A I T S O H G H
N B V O O D O O C
```

All the words are hidden vertically, horizontally, or diagonally, in both directions. The letters that remain unused form a key word when read in order.

MEDIUM

				7		2		
							3	
			6			5		
		6		2				
	7	9					4	
	4		3	9				7
	8		5		7	1		
5		2		4	8	7		9
6		7	9			4	8	

*Fill in the grid so that each row, each column,
and each 3x3 frame contains every number from 1 to 9.*

MEDIUM

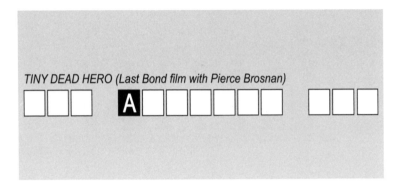

TINY DEAD HERO (Last Bond film with Pierce Brosnan)

☐☐☐ **A**☐☐☐☐☐ ☐☐☐

ALIEN CAR (Played Bond in 'Skyfall')

D☐☐**I**☐☐ ☐☐☐**G**

Form the word or phrase that is described in parentheses with the letters above the grid. Extra letters are already in the right place.

EASY

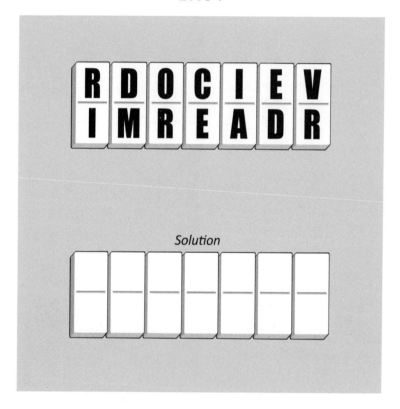

Solution

Move the letter blocks around to form words on top
and below that you can associate with **opposite**.

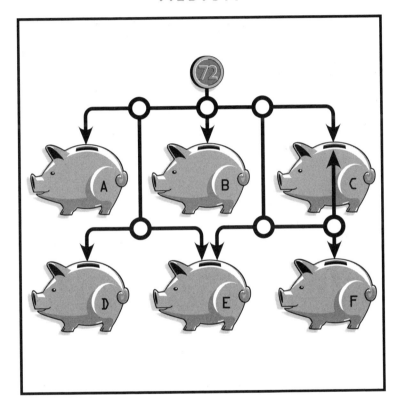

*Which piggy bank (A-F) will receive the largest
amount of the 72 dollars, knowing that the money
is divided proportionally when split up?*

MEDIUM

5	2	2	4	●	5
5	2	②	4	3	1
5	1	0	1	3	3
1	3	1	3	4	4
2	2	2	3	2	1
2	3	5	2	1	2

Draw the shortest path from the ball to the hole. You can only move along vertical and horizontal lines. The figure on each square indicates the number of squares the ball must move in the same direction. You can change direction at each stop.

HARD

N A V I G A T E

-A

| | I | | | | |

G R E N A D E S

+E

r e n e g **A** d e s

The word below contains the letters of the word
above plus or minus the letter in the middle.
One letter is already in the right place.

EASY

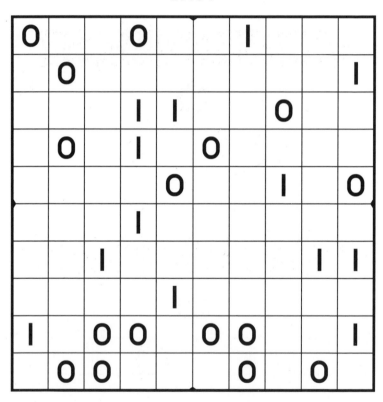

Complete the grid with zeros and ones until there are five zeros
and five ones in every row and every column. No more than two
of the same number can be next to or under each other. Rows
or columns with exactly the same content are not allowed.

MEDIUM

(1) before noon

(2) human limb

(3) planet

(4) wise

(5) academic degree

(6) composer

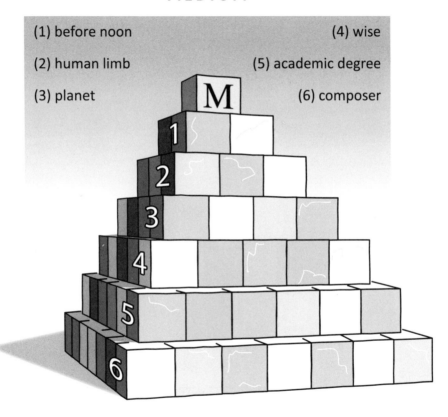

*Each word in the pyramid has the letters of
the word above it, plus a new letter.*

HARD

*What word or concept
is depicted here?*

EASY

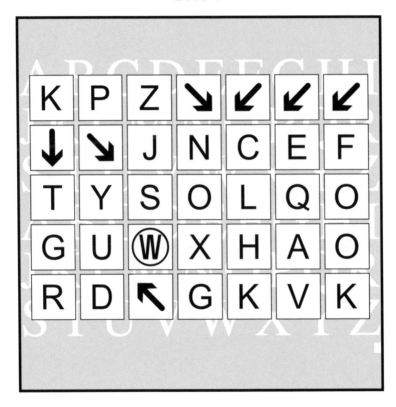

Knowing that every arrow points to a letter and that no letter can touch another vertically, horizontally, or diagonally, find the missing letters that form a key word when read in order. We show one letter in a circle to help you get started.

EASY

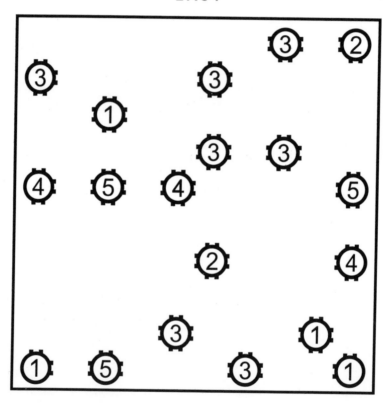

Link all circles with straight horizontal or vertical lines into one connected group. The numbers tell how many lines are connected to a circle. There can be no more than two lines in the same direction and lines cannot cross circles or other lines.

MEDIUM

APPLAUSE
BANG
BLAST
CHANGE
DEAF
EARDRUM
GONG
HERTZ
LOW
MUFFLE
SONG
SPEED
TALK
THRESHOLD
THUNDER

F	G	N	A	B	S	M	O	U
A	A	P	P	L	A	U	S	E
E	E	N	E	O	D	R	Z	R
D	L	T	G	W	T	D	T	E
S	F	S	N	S	A	R	R	D
P	F	A	A	O	L	A	E	N
E	U	L	H	N	K	E	H	U
E	M	B	C	G	O	N	G	H
D	L	O	H	S	E	R	H	T

All the words are hidden vertically, horizontally, or diagonally, in both directions. The letters that remain unused form a key word when read in order.

HARD

	7		1	2	4		5	8
	1			8				
		2	9			6		
				9			6	4
	3				5		9	
6		9				1		
8							4	
		5	2				8	3

*Fill in the grid so that each row, each column,
and each 3x3 frame contains every number from 1 to 9.*

MEDIUM

RANSOMS (arise when a strong wind blows loose sand)

| | | | **D** | | | **T** | | | |

MERMAID INN (heat wave in the autumn)

| | | | | | | | **S** | **U** | | | |

Form the word or phrase that is described in parentheses with the letters above the grid. Extra letters are already in the right place.

MEDIUM

Solution

*Move the letter blocks around to form words on top
and below that you can associate with **electricity**.
The letters are reversed on one block.*

MEDIUM

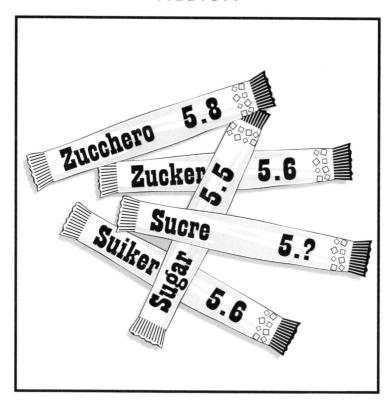

The weight of sugar is different per country. Which number should replace the question mark on the 'Sucre' packet?

MEDIUM

5	2	5	3	3	5
1	3	2	4	3	1
2	4	2	2	2	4
5	2	0	0	4	
4	1	4	1	3	3
5	2	1	1	4	4

Draw the shortest path from the ball to the hole. You can only move along vertical and horizontal lines. The figure on each square indicates the number of squares the ball must move in the same direction. You can change direction at each stop.

HARD

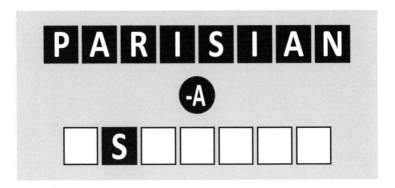

P A R I S I A N

-A

□ S □ □ □ □ □

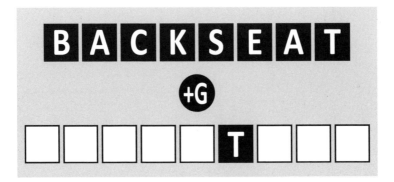

B A C K S E A T

+G

□ □ □ □ □ T □ □ □

The word below contains the letters of the word above plus or minus the letter in the middle. One letter is already in the right place.

121

MEDIUM

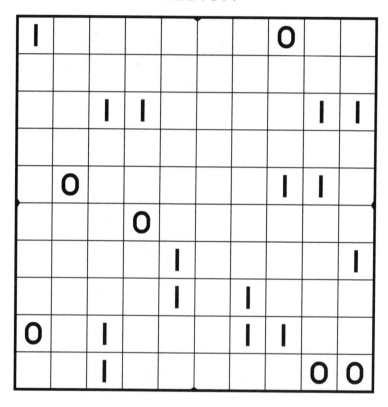

*Complete the grid with zeros and ones until there are five zeros
and five ones in every row and every column. No more than two
of the same number can be next to or under each other. Rows
or columns with exactly the same content are not allowed.*

Word Pyramid

MEDIUM

(1) South East

(2) group of things

(3) 10s

(4) rear part of a ship

(5) put in

(6) cocktail of crème de menthe and brandy

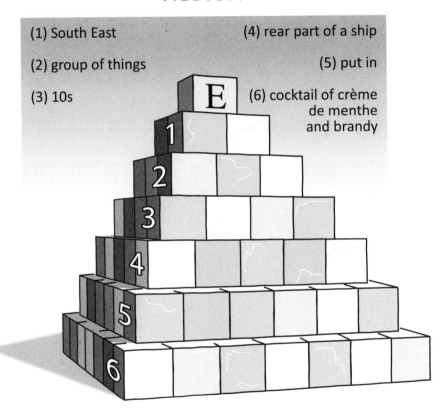

Each word in the pyramid has the letters of the word above it, plus a new letter.

HARD

*What word or concept
is depicted here?*

Find The Word

MEDIUM

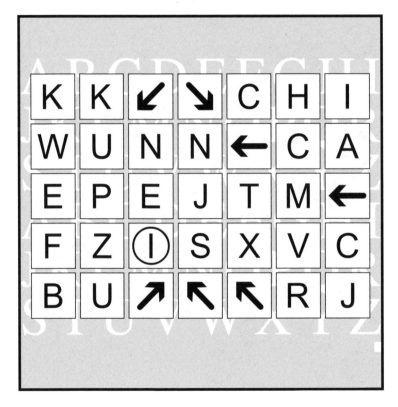

Knowing that every arrow points to a letter and that no letter can touch another vertically, horizontally, or diagonally, find the missing letters that form a key word when read in order. We show one letter in a circle to help you get started.

MEDIUM

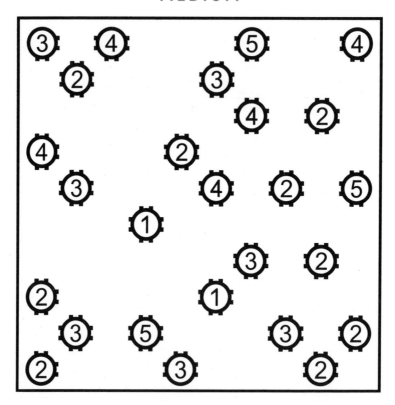

Link all circles with straight horizontal or vertical lines into one connected group. The numbers tell how many lines are connected to a circle. There can be no more than two lines in the same direction and lines cannot cross circles or other lines.

MEDIUM

ATONAL
BALLAD
CANTILENA
COPLA
ELEGY
HYMN
IDYLL
MADRIGAL
OCTET
ODE
PROSE
RIDDLE
SATIRE
SONNET
STANZA

S	T	A	N	Z	A	P	L	O
H	L	A	N	O	T	A	A	E
O	Y	C	O	P	L	A	G	R
C	E	M	L	L	Y	D	I	I
T	E	N	N	O	S	D	R	T
E	S	O	R	P	D	T	D	A
T	D	A	L	L	A	B	A	S
E	Y	G	E	L	E	R	M	Y
C	A	N	T	I	L	E	N	A

All the words are hidden vertically, horizontally, or diagonally, in both directions. The letters that remain unused form a key word when read in order.

Sudoku

VERY HARD

	2		7				4	3
5				4	6	9	2	
			5					7
		8					1	4
		7				2		
9	3						6	
	8	1		2	9			
		9	1					
			3					

Fill in the grid so that each row, each column,
and each 3x3 frame contains every number from 1 to 9.

MEDIUM

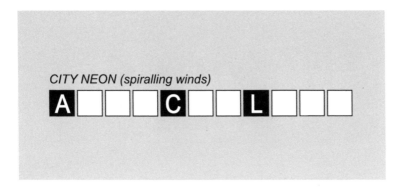

CITY NEON (spiralling winds)

A _ _ _ C _ _ L _ _ _

NO GOLD (inundation of areas)

F _ _ _ _ I _ _

Form the word or phrase that is described in parentheses with the letters above the grid. Extra letters are already in the right place.

HARD

Solution

Move the letter blocks around to form words on top and below that you can associate with **school courses**. The letters are reversed on two blocks.

HARD

Which mushroom (1-7) does not belong?

Golf Maze

MEDIUM

4	4	5	3	5	4
5	3	1	4	3	1
2	1	0	3	3	
2	4	1	2	2	3
5	2	2	2	1	1
2	1	1	5	1	1

Draw the shortest path from the ball to the hole. You can only move along vertical and horizontal lines. The figure on each square indicates the number of squares the ball must move in the same direction. You can change direction at each stop.

HARD

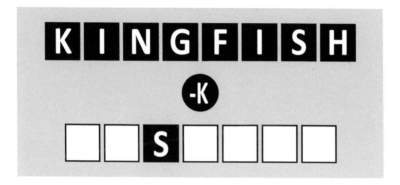

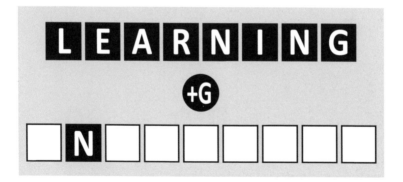

*The word below contains the letters of the word
above plus or minus the letter in the middle.
One letter is already in the right place.*

HARD

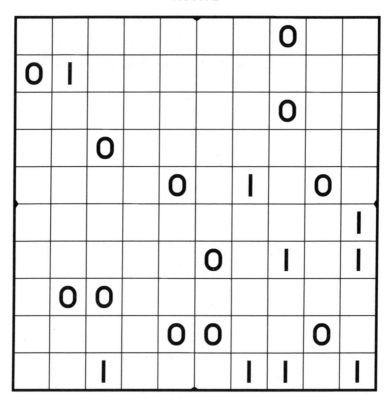

Complete the grid with zeros and ones until there are five zeros and five ones in every row and every column. No more than two of the same number can be next to or under each other. Rows or columns with exactly the same content are not allowed.

MEDIUM

(1) to the same degree

(2) pitiful

(3) serious disease of the immune system

(4) thoughts

(5) suggest

(6) infests

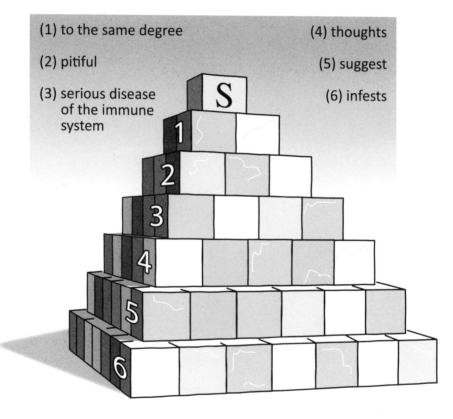

Each word in the pyramid has the letters of the word above it, plus a new letter.

*What word or concept
is depicted here?*

HARD

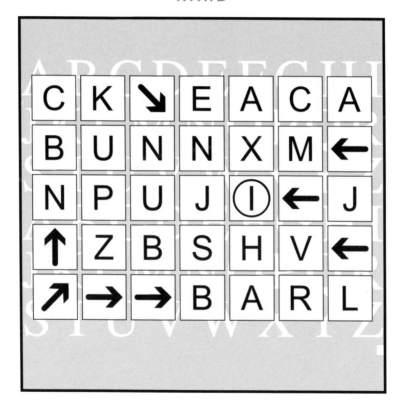

C	K	↘	E	A	C	A
B	U	N	N	X	M	←
N	P	U	J	Ⓘ	←	J
↑	Z	B	S	H	V	←
↗	→	→	B	A	R	L

Knowing that every arrow points to a letter and that no letter can touch another vertically, horizontally, or diagonally, find the missing letters that form a key word when read in order. We show one letter in a circle to help you get started.

HARD

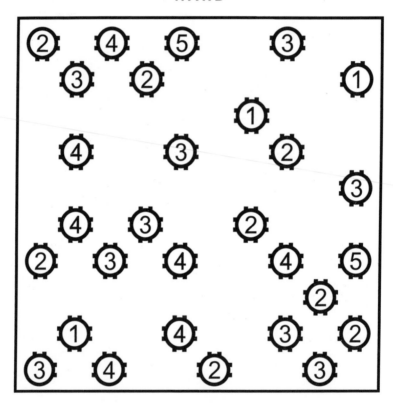

Link all circles with straight horizontal or vertical lines into one connected group. The numbers tell how many lines are connected to a circle. There can be no more than two lines in the same direction and lines cannot cross circles or other lines.

Word Search

CHILLY
COLD
FIRE
FROST
GALE
GLOVES
HAT
ICE
IGLOO
MISTLETOE
SALT
SCARF
SEASON
SHIVER
SKI
SNOW
STEW

S	H	I	V	E	R	T	M	F
S	W	O	N	S	A	I	I	T
S	K	W	O	H	C	R	S	G
C	Y	I	S	E	E	O	T	L
A	L	O	A	I	R	N	L	O
R	L	O	E	F	D	T	E	V
F	I	L	S	S	A	L	T	E
E	H	G	W	E	T	S	O	S
R	C	I	G	A	L	E	E	C

All the words are hidden vertically, horizontally, or diagonally, in both directions. The letters that remain unused form a key word when read in order.

EASY

6		3			8	1	9	2
5	9	2	1	4				
	8	7					4	6
4			6		5	2		
	5		9	7			3	4
		8						1
			8		9	7		
	1				4			
							6	

Fill in the grid so that each row, each column,
and each 3x3 frame contains every number from 1 to 9.

MEDIUM

MIDSTREAM *(someone who has exceptional intellectual ability)*

☐ ☐ ☐ ☐ ☐ ☐ ☐ ☐ **N** ☐

MY POOL *(market in which there is only one seller)*

☐ ☐ **N** ☐ ☐ **O** ☐ ☐

Form the word or phrase that is described in parentheses with the letters above the grid. Extra letters are already in the right place.

EASY

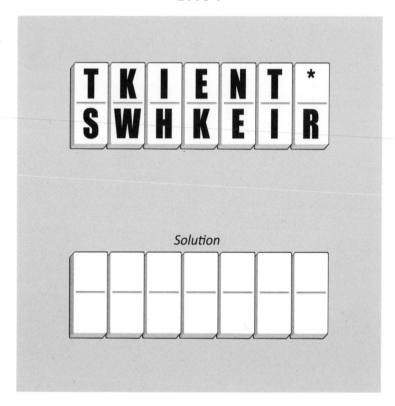

Solution

Move the letter blocks around to form words on top
and below that you can associate with **cat**.

How cold is it on the highest mountaintop?

Golf Maze

MEDIUM

5	3	5	4	3	1
2	1	1	4	0	4
2	2	3	2	3	4
1	4	1	2	1	4
5	4	1	3	2	5
1	5	2	5	3	

Draw the shortest path from the ball to the hole. You can only move along vertical and horizontal lines. The figure on each square indicates the number of squares the ball must move in the same direction. You can change direction at each stop.

HARD

BARGAINS

-B

		N			

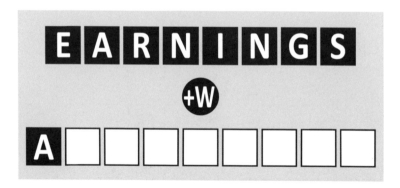

EARNINGS

+W

A							

*The word below contains the letters of the word
above plus or minus the letter in the middle.
One letter is already in the right place.*

EASY

				I		I	O		
			I						
		I					I		I
	I		O						I
			O		O		I	I	
							I		
I		O				O			
				O					I
		I					O		I	I
O	I	I				O		O	

Complete the grid with zeros and ones until there are five zeros and five ones in every row and every column. No more than two of the same number can be next to or under each other. Rows or columns with exactly the same content are not allowed.

Word Pyramid

(1) point in time

(2) insect living in organized colonies

(3) volcano in Sicily

(4) broker

(5) feeding

(6) make hot

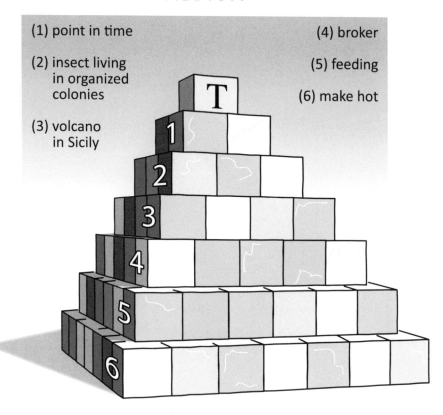

Each word in the pyramid has the letters of the word above it, plus a new letter.

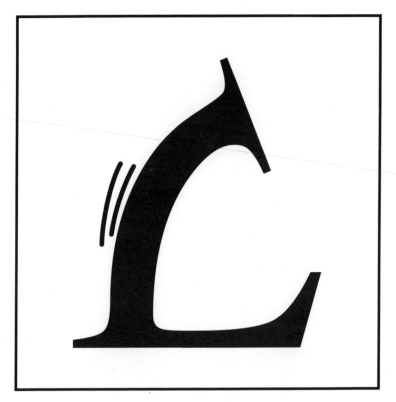

*What word or concept
is depicted here?*

Find The Word

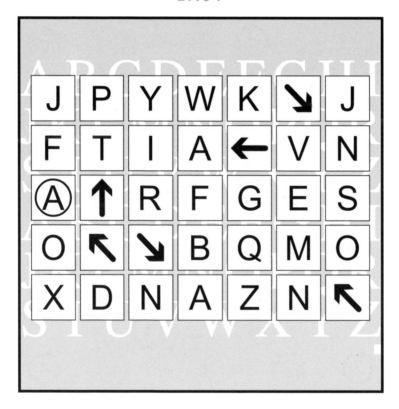

Knowing that every arrow points to a letter and that no letter can touch another vertically, horizontally, or diagonally, find the missing letters that form a key word when read in order. We show one letter in a circle to help you get started.

EASY

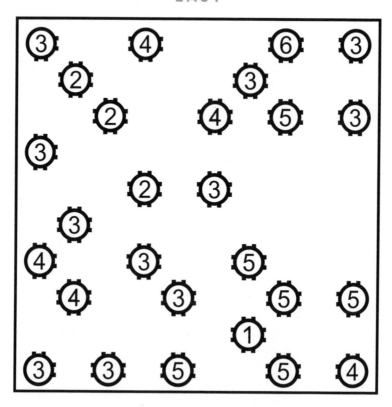

Link all circles with straight horizontal or vertical lines into
one connected group. The numbers tell how many lines are
connected to a circle. There can be no more than two lines in
the same direction and lines cannot cross circles or other lines.

Word Search

BROOCH
CARAT
CHAIN
CLASP
CROWN
CRYSTAL
GOLD
MEDAILLON
NECKLACE
PEARL
PIN
SHINE
SILVER
TIARA
WATCH

N	A	R	A	I	T	J	T	N
W	W	E	G	W	B	A	L	O
E	A	O	L	E	R	S	A	L
E	L	T	R	A	O	I	T	L
D	N	R	C	C	O	L	S	I
R	N	I	A	H	C	V	Y	A
N	I	P	H	E	H	E	R	D
Y	C	L	A	S	P	R	C	E
E	C	A	L	K	C	E	N	M

*All the words are hidden vertically, horizontally,
or diagonally, in both directions. The letters that remain
unused form a key word when read in order.*

MEDIUM

	9	6			3		8	
7			6				4	5
		8	1	7	9		6	3
		9	3		5	7	2	
5			2	6				
				4		5		6
	2						3	
	6							9
						4		

Fill in the grid so that each row, each column,
and each 3x3 frame contains every number from 1 to 9.

Anagrams

TOASTER *(board game for two players on a 10×10 square board)*

						G	

OUTLET *(machine with a revolving toothed wheel)*

R				E		

Form the word or phrase that is described in parentheses with the letters above the grid. Extra letters are already in the right place.

MEDIUM

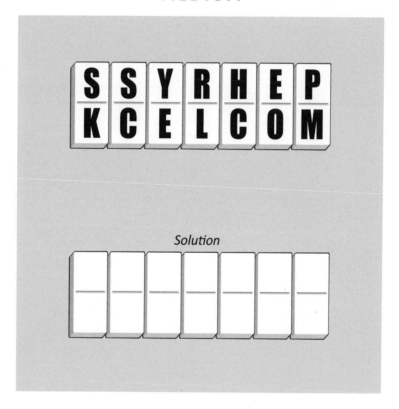

Solution

Move the letter blocks around to form words on top and
below that you can associate with **coniferous trees**.
The letters are reversed on one block.

MEDIUM

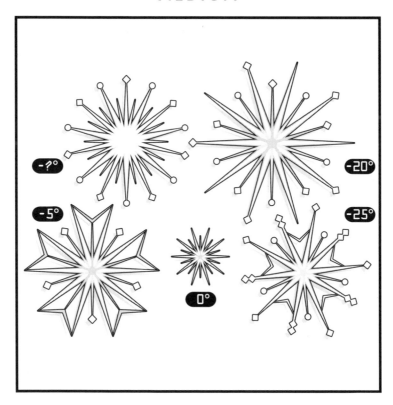

*Every freezing temperature creates a different ice crystal.
Which temperature would result in the crystal with the question
mark, knowing that only the squares and circles are important?*

Golf Maze

MEDIUM

2	1	5	4	5	4
2	0	4	1	1	1
2	4	1	2	2	3
2	2	2	3	4	1
1		3	1	2	1
2	3	2	5	1	2

Draw the shortest path from the ball to the hole. You can only move along vertical and horizontal lines. The figure on each square indicates the number of squares the ball must move in the same direction. You can change direction at each stop.

HARD

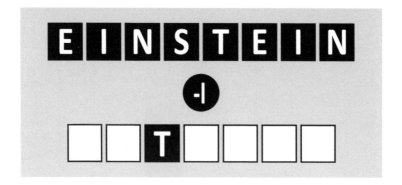

The word below contains the letters of the word above plus or minus the letter in the middle. One letter is already in the right place.

Binairo®

MEDIUM

O						O	I		
							O		
		I	I			O			
					O		I		
				I					
			I	I					I
O			I						I
		O				I		I	
						I			I
	O							I	I

Complete the grid with zeros and ones until there are five zeros and five ones in every row and every column. No more than two of the same number can be next to or under each other. Rows or columns with exactly the same content are not allowed.

MEDIUM

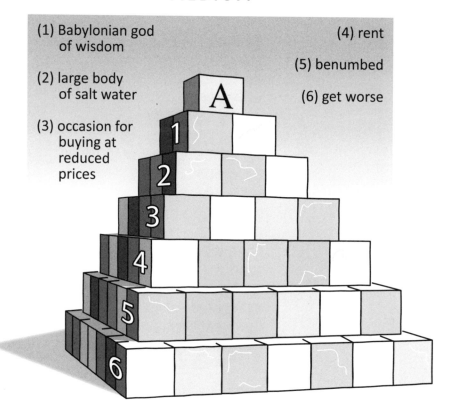

(1) Babylonian god of wisdom

(2) large body of salt water

(3) occasion for buying at reduced prices

(4) rent

(5) benumbed

(6) get worse

Each word in the pyramid has the letters of the word above it, plus a new letter.

MEDIUM

*What word or concept
is depicted here?*

MEDIUM

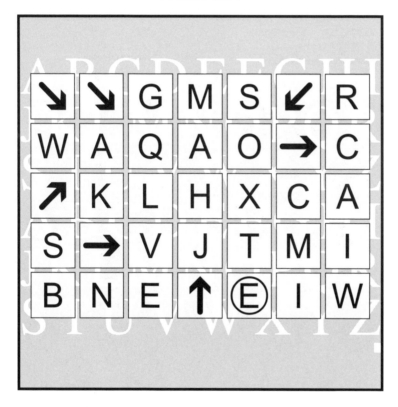

Knowing that every arrow points to a letter and that no letter can touch another vertically, horizontally, or diagonally, find the missing letters that form a key word when read in order. We show one letter in a circle to help you get started.

MEDIUM

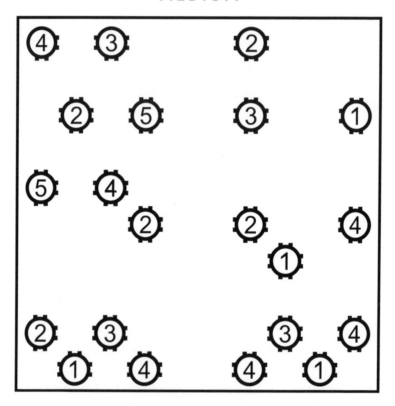

Link all circles with straight horizontal or vertical lines into one connected group. The numbers tell how many lines are connected to a circle. There can be no more than two lines in the same direction and lines cannot cross circles or other lines.

If you can't solve certain puzzles, don't look up the answers — just try again later.

Finding the solution is much more fun than knowing the solution.

page 7
NEW YORK

page 8

8	5	2	3	9	6	7	1	4
6	3	7	4	1	5	9	8	2
4	9	1	8	7	2	5	6	3
5	4	3	2	8	1	6	7	9
2	1	9	7	6	4	3	5	8
7	6	8	5	3	9	2	4	1
1	2	4	6	5	3	8	9	7
3	8	5	9	4	7	1	2	6
9	7	6	1	2	8	4	3	5

page 9
BICYCLE RACING
FIGURE SKATING

page 10
HOSTING
NETWORK

page 11
E. The cyclists always ride to cities where the first letters form TOUR DE FRANCE.

page 12

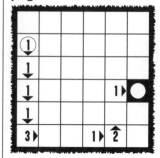

page 13
DECADES
STRIKEOUT

page 14

1	1	0	0	1	0	1	0	1	0
0	1	1	0	1	0	1	0	1	0
1	0	0	1	0	1	0	1	0	1
1	0	0	1	0	0	1	0	1	1
0	1	1	0	1	0	0	1	1	0
1	0	0	1	0	1	1	0	0	1
0	1	1	0	0	1	0	1	0	1
1	0	0	1	1	0	1	0	1	0
0	1	1	0	1	1	0	1	0	0
0	0	1	1	0	1	0	1	0	1

page 15
(1) IS
(2) SIR
(3) RISK
(4) SKIRT
(5) TRIKES
(6) STRIKES

page 16
ten SE = TENNESSEE

page 17
DANCING

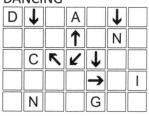

page 18

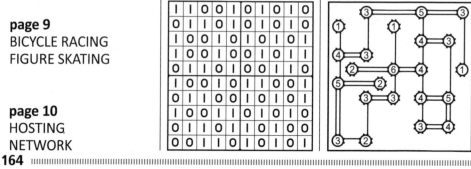

page 19
GARDEN

page 20

9	1	5	4	6	7	3	2	8
6	3	8	2	1	5	9	7	4
2	7	4	3	8	9	5	1	6
5	4	6	7	9	2	8	3	1
1	2	3	8	4	6	7	5	9
7	8	9	5	3	1	4	6	2
4	9	1	6	7	3	2	8	5
8	5	7	1	2	4	6	9	3
3	6	2	9	5	8	1	4	7

page 21
ACADEMY AWARD
MERYL STREEP

page 22
ASPIRIN
SURGERY

page 23
Pattern 2. The shapes in the pattern shift 1 step down and the bottom shape is placed on top, then they shift 2 steps down, then 3 and finally 4 steps. Since there are only four shapes, the pattern is the same as the previous one.

page 24

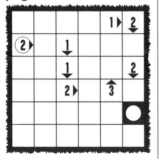

page 25
WELFARE
DIPLOMACY

page 26

I	0	I	0	I	0	I	I	0	0
0	I	0	I	0	I	I	0	0	I
0	0	I	I	0	I	0	0	I	I
I	I	0	0	I	0	0	I	I	0
I	I	0	0	I	0	I	0	0	I
0	0	I	I	0	I	0	I	I	0
0	I	0	0	I	0	I	0	I	I
I	0	I	I	0	0	I	I	0	0
0	I	0	I	0	I	0	0	I	I
I	0	I	0	I	I	0	I	0	0

page 27
(1) TO
(2) LOT
(3) LOST
(4) STOLE
(5) HOSTEL
(6) HOLSTER

page 28
ring T on E = RINGTONE

page 29
WARNING

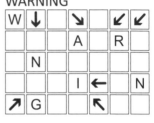

page 30

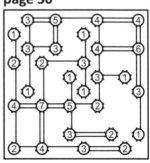

page 31
FASTFOOD

page 32

9	2	6	1	5	8	3	7	4
3	7	8	4	9	6	2	1	5
4	5	1	2	3	7	9	6	8
6	3	7	5	8	4	1	9	2
8	9	4	3	1	2	6	5	7
2	1	5	7	6	9	4	8	3
5	4	2	9	7	1	8	3	6
1	8	3	6	2	5	7	4	9
7	6	9	8	4	3	5	2	1

page 33
JACK NICHOLSON
KATHARINE HEPBURN

page 34
AIRPORT
LUGGAGE

page 35
Five people. Four oarsmen and a coxswain. You can discover this because there is not an extra oar visible at the front of the top image.

page 36

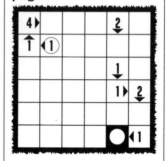

page 37
DAILIES
AMERICANS

page 38

I	O	I	I	O	O	I	O	O	I
O	I	I	O	O	I	O	I	O	I
I	I	O	O	I	O	I	O	I	O
I	O	O	I	I	O	O	I	I	O
O	O	I	I	O	I	I	O	O	I
O	I	O	O	I	O	I	O	I	I
I	I	O	I	O	I	O	I	O	O
O	O	I	O	I	O	I	O	I	I
O	O	I	I	O	I	O	I	I	O
I	I	O	O	I	I	O	I	O	O

page 39
(1) AD
(2) LAD
(3) LAID
(4) IDEAL
(5) LADIES
(6) MISLEAD

page 40
M asks = MASKS

page 41
JACKPOT

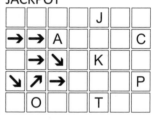

page 42

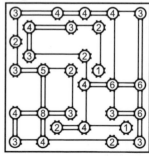

page 43
CALIFORNIA

page 44

5	8	3	9	6	4	7	2	1
7	6	1	2	5	3	9	4	8
2	9	4	7	8	1	3	5	6
1	5	9	8	2	7	4	6	3
3	4	7	1	9	6	2	8	5
6	2	8	4	3	5	1	7	9
9	3	2	5	7	8	6	1	4
8	1	6	3	4	2	5	9	7
4	7	5	6	1	9	8	3	2

page 45
WASHINGTON
MISSOURI

page 46
ANATOMY
HABITAT

page 47
Kebab 5. All other kebabs start and end with a sausage.

page 48

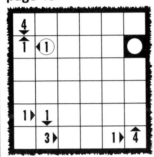

page 49
LANDING
CONTAINER

page 50

I	0	I	0	I	0	I	0	I	0
0	I	0	0	I	I	0	I	0	I
0	0	I	I	0	I	0	0	I	I
I	0	0	I	I	0	I	0	I	0
0	I	0	0	I	0	I	I	0	I
I	0	I	I	0	I	0	I	0	0
I	I	0	I	0	0	I	0	I	0
0	I	I	0	I	0	0	I	0	I
0	0	I	0	0	I	I	0	I	I
I	I	0	I	0	I	0	I	0	0

page 51
(1) MD
(2) MAD
(3) MADE
(4) MEDIA
(5) ADMIRE
(6) MERMAID

page 52
S cape = ESCAPE

page 53
GAMBLER

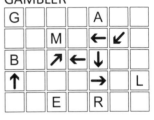

page 54

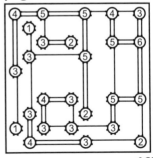

page 55
CHILDREN

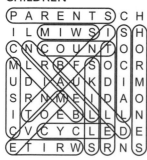

page 56

2	5	4	3	1	9	6	8	7
7	9	6	5	8	2	3	4	1
1	3	8	6	7	4	5	9	2
4	6	7	1	2	5	8	3	9
5	8	1	9	6	3	2	7	4
9	2	3	8	4	7	1	5	6
6	7	5	2	9	8	4	1	3
8	1	9	4	3	6	7	2	5
3	4	2	7	5	1	9	6	8

page 57
RHODE ISLAND
DELAWARE

page 58
AMAZON
ORINOCO

page 59
A. Read as follows: the second and second last letter of the previous port are the first and last letter of the next port.

page 60

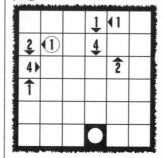

page 61
MALARIA
LIFEGUARD

page 62

0	0	I	I	0	I	0	0	I	I
0	I	I	0	0	I	0	I	I	0
I	I	0	0	I	0	I	I	0	0
I	0	0	I	I	0	I	0	0	I
0	0	I	I	0	I	0	I	I	0
I	I	0	0	I	I	0	I	0	0
0	0	I	0	I	0	I	0	I	I
I	I	0	I	0	0	I	0	I	0
0	0	I	I	0	I	0	I	0	I
I	I	0	0	I	0	I	0	0	I

page 63
(1) RE
(2) EAR
(3) DEAR
(4) GRADE
(5) DANGER
(6) READING

page 64
f email = FEMALE

page 65
YANKEES

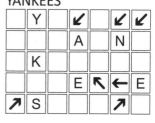

page 66

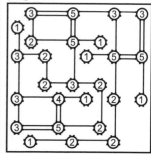

page 67
THEATRE

page 68

5	4	6	3	8	7	9	2	1
7	9	1	6	2	4	5	3	8
3	8	2	9	5	1	6	7	4
2	6	9	8	1	3	7	4	5
1	7	5	4	9	2	8	6	3
8	3	4	7	6	5	1	9	2
6	2	8	5	4	9	3	1	7
9	1	3	2	7	8	4	5	6
4	5	7	1	3	6	2	8	9

page 69
GREYHOUND
BLUE WHALE

page 70
STABLE
TRACTOR

page 71
0. On all the other faces the features are formed by two numbers whose sum equals six.

page 72

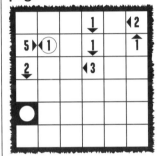

page 73
SEGMENT
HOUSEMAID

page 74

I	0	0	I	0	I	0	I	I	0
0	I	0	I	I	0	0	I	I	0
I	0	I	0	I	0	I	0	0	I
0	I	I	0	0	I	0	I	I	0
I	0	0	I	I	0	I	I	0	0
0	I	I	0	0	I	0	0	I	I
I	I	0	I	0	0	I	0	0	I
0	0	I	0	I	I	0	I	I	0
I	0	0	I	I	0	I	0	0	I
0	I	I	0	0	I	I	0	0	I

page 75
(1) BE
(2) BEL
(3) ABLE
(4) TABLE
(5) STABLE
(6) BATTLES

page 76
BREAKDOWN

page 77
LAUNDRY

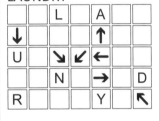

page 78

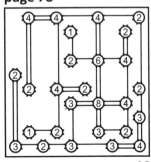

page 79
ANATOMY

page 80

8	9	4	6	7	2	3	5	1
3	7	5	9	8	1	6	2	4
1	2	6	4	5	3	8	7	9
4	1	7	5	6	9	2	3	8
2	8	9	1	3	7	4	6	5
6	5	3	2	4	8	1	9	7
7	6	1	3	9	4	5	8	2
9	3	2	8	1	5	7	4	6
5	4	8	7	2	6	9	1	3

page 81
RED KANGAROO
BENGAL TIGER

page 82
PARTNER
WEDDING

page 83
Piece 4. Only the pieces 2, 4 and 6 consist of the 10 blocks that you need to complete the cube. Only piece 4 has the right shape and the right colors.

page 84

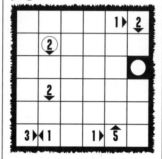

page 85
CATTAIL
COUNTRIES

page 86

0	I	0	I	0	I	I	0	I	0
I	0	I	0	I	0	I	0	I	0
I	I	0	0	I	0	0	I	0	I
0	0	I	I	0	I	0	I	I	0
0	I	0	0	I	0	I	0	I	I
I	0	I	I	0	I	0	I	0	0
0	0	I	I	0	0	I	I	0	I
I	I	0	0	I	I	0	0	I	0
0	I	I	0	0	I	0	I	0	I
I	0	0	I	I	0	I	0	0	I

page 87
(1) FA
(2) FAR
(3) RAFT
(4) AFTER
(5) FATHER
(6) FEATHER

page 88
CATE ring = CATERING

page 89
ICEPICK

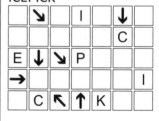

page 90

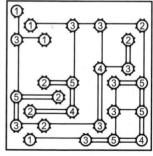

page 91
PICASSO

page 92

8	6	3	1	7	4	5	9	2
2	9	4	8	5	6	1	3	7
7	1	5	2	9	3	6	4	8
9	2	8	7	1	5	4	6	3
4	5	7	3	6	9	8	2	1
6	3	1	4	2	8	9	7	5
1	7	6	5	4	2	3	8	9
5	8	9	6	3	7	2	1	4
3	4	2	9	8	1	7	5	6

page 93
LIVE AND LET DIE
TIMOTHY DALTON

page 94
KETCHUP
MUSTARD

page 95
Car 11. All white and black cars are parked nose inward. All gray cars are parked with the nose outward, except car 11.

page 96

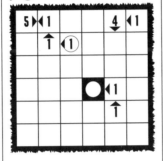

page 97
STRANGE
DRUMBEATS

page 98

0	I	I	0	0	I	I	0	0	I
I	0	I	0	I	I	0	0	I	0
0	I	0	I	I	0	I	I	0	0
0	I	0	I	0	I	0	I	0	I
I	0	I	0	I	0	I	0	I	0
I	I	0	I	0	0	I	0	0	I
0	0	I	I	0	I	0	I	I	0
I	I	0	0	I	0	0	I	0	I
0	0	I	0	I	0	I	0	I	I
I	0	0	I	0	I	0	I	I	0

page 99
(1) IT
(2) SIT
(3) SPIT
(4) STRIP
(5) PRIEST
(6) PIRATES

page 100
HEADLINE

page 101
AVOCADO

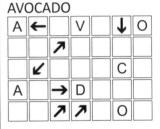

page 102

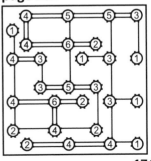

page 103
HORROR

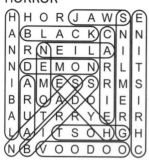

page 104

8	9	5	4	7	3	2	1	6
7	6	1	2	8	5	9	3	4
4	2	3	6	1	9	5	7	8
3	5	6	7	2	4	8	9	1
1	7	9	8	5	6	3	4	2
2	4	8	3	9	1	6	5	7
9	8	4	5	6	7	1	2	3
5	3	2	1	4	8	7	6	9
6	1	7	9	3	2	4	8	5

page 105
DIE ANOTHER DAY
DANIEL CRAIG

page 106
DIVORCE
MARRIED

page 107
B. Piggy bank B always receives 1/3 of 24. All the other piggy banks receive less. A: 12, C: 15, D: 6, E: 12 and F: 3.

page 108

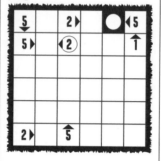

page 109
VINTAGE
RENEGADES

page 110

0	I	I	0	0	I	I	0	I	0
I	0	I	0	0	I	0	I	0	I
0	I	0	I	I	0	I	0	I	0
I	0	0	I	I	0	I	0	0	I
0	I	I	0	0	I	0	I	I	0
I	0	0	I	I	0	I	I	0	0
0	0	I	I	0	I	0	0	I	I
0	I	I	0	I	0	I	0	I	0
I	I	0	0	I	0	0	I	0	I
I	0	0	I	0	I	0	I	0	I

page 111
(1) A.M.
(2) ARM
(3) MARS
(4) SMART
(5) MASTER
(6) MAESTRO

page 112
CHAIRMAN

page 113
NETWORK

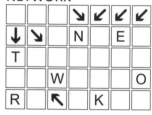

page 114

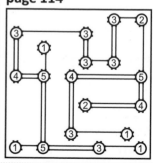

page 115
SOUND

page 116

9	7	6	1	2	4	3	5	8
5	1	3	7	8	6	4	2	9
4	8	2	9	5	3	6	1	7
2	5	8	3	9	1	7	6	4
7	3	1	4	6	5	8	9	2
6	4	9	8	7	2	1	3	5
8	2	7	6	3	9	5	4	1
1	6	5	2	4	7	9	8	3
3	9	4	5	1	8	2	7	6

page 117
SANDSTORM
INDIAN SUMMER

page 118
DYNAMO
BATTERY

page 119
5. The number after the decimal point is equal to the number of letters in the name on the sugar packet.

page 120

page 121
ASPIRIN
BACKSTAGE

page 122

I	I	O	I	O	O	I	O	O	I
I	I	O	O	I	O	O	I	I	O
O	O	I	I	O	I	O	O	I	I
O	I	I	O	O	I	I	O	O	I
I	O	O	I	I	O	O	I	I	O
I	O	I	O	O	I	I	O	I	O
O	I	O	O	I	I	O	I	O	I
I	O	O	I	I	O	I	O	I	O
O	O	I	I	O	O	I	I	O	I
O	I	I	O	I	I	O	I	O	O

page 123
(1) SE
(2) SET
(3) TENS
(4) STERN
(5) INSERT
(6) STINGER

page 124
L on DON = LONDON

page 125
KINETIC

page 126

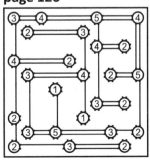

page 127
POETRY

page 128

8	2	6	7	9	1	5	4	3
5	7	3	8	4	6	9	2	1
1	9	4	3	5	2	6	8	7
2	6	8	9	7	5	3	1	4
4	1	7	6	8	3	2	9	5
9	3	5	2	1	4	7	6	8
7	8	1	5	2	9	4	3	6
3	4	9	1	6	7	8	5	2
6	5	2	4	3	8	1	7	9

page 129
ANTICYCLONE
FLOODING

page 130
HISTORY
PHYSICS

page 131
Mushroom 5. All the other mushrooms have the same white spots in the same place.

page 132

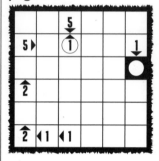

page 133
FISHING
ENLARGING

page 134

I	O	I	O	I	I	O	O	I	O
O	I	O	I	I	O	O	I	I	O
O	O	I	I	O	I	I	O	O	I
I	I	O	O	I	I	O	O	I	O
I	I	O	I	O	O	I	I	O	O
O	O	I	O	O	I	I	O	I	I
O	I	I	O	I	O	O	I	O	I
I	O	O	I	O	I	O	I	I	O
I	I	O	I	O	O	I	O	O	I
O	O	I	O	I	O	I	I	O	I

page 135
(1) AS
(2) SAD
(3) AIDS
(4) IDEAS
(5) ADVISE
(6) INVADES

page 136
COMPOST

page 137
CANNIBAL

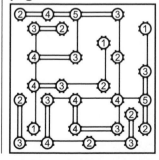

page 138

page 139
WINTER

page 140

6	4	3	7	5	8	1	9	2
5	9	2	1	4	6	3	8	7
1	8	7	2	9	3	5	4	6
4	3	1	6	8	5	2	7	9
2	5	6	9	7	1	8	3	4
9	7	8	4	3	2	6	5	1
3	6	4	8	2	9	7	1	5
7	1	5	3	6	4	9	2	8
8	2	9	5	1	7	4	6	3

page 141
MASTERMIND
MONOPOLY

page 142
KITTEN
WHISKER

page 143
-2. The freezing temperature in each zone is equal to the number of snowflakes.

page 144

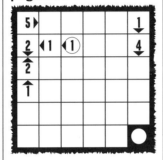

page 145
SANGRIA
ANSWERING

page 146

I	I	0	0	I	0	I	0	I	0
I	0	0	I	I	0	I	0	I	0
0	0	I	I	0	I	0	I	0	I
0	I	I	0	0	I	I	0	0	I
I	I	0	0	I	0	0	I	I	0
0	0	I	I	0	0	I	I	0	I
I	I	0	0	I	I	0	0	I	0
I	0	0	I	0	0	I	I	0	I
0	0	I	I	0	I	0	0	I	I
0	I	I	0	I	I	0	I	0	0

page 147
(1) AT
(2) ANT
(3) ETNA
(4) AGENT
(5) EATING
(6) HEATING

page 148
ELBOW

page 149
PANAMA

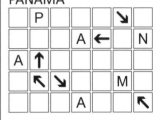

page 150

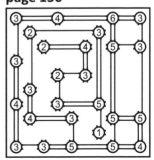

page 151
JEWELERY

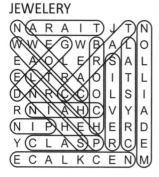

page 152

2	9	6	4	5	3	1	8	7
7	3	1	6	2	8	9	4	5
4	5	8	1	7	9	2	6	3
6	1	9	3	8	5	7	2	4
5	4	7	2	6	1	3	9	8
3	8	2	9	4	7	5	1	6
8	2	5	7	9	4	6	3	1
1	6	4	5	3	2	8	7	9
9	7	3	8	1	6	4	5	2

page 153
STRATEGO
ROULETTE

page 154
CYPRESS
HEMLOCK

page 155
- 21°. Every square has a value of -1° and every circle has a value of -2°.

page 156

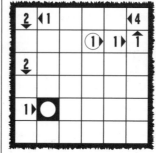

page 157
INTENSE
ECONOMIST

page 158

0	1	1	0	1	0	0	1	1	0
1	1	0	0	1	1	0	1	0	0
0	0	1	1	0	1	1	0	0	1
1	0	1	1	0	0	1	0	1	0
0	1	0	0	1	1	0	1	1	0
1	0	0	1	1	0	1	0	0	1
0	0	1	1	0	1	0	1	0	1
1	1	0	0	1	0	1	0	1	0
0	1	0	1	0	0	1	1	0	1
1	0	1	0	0	1	0	0	1	1

page 159
(1) EA
(2) SEA
(3) SALE
(4) LEASE
(5) ASLEEP
(6) RELAPSE

page 160
T cups = TEACUPS

page 161
MACHINE

↘	↘		M		↙	
	A				→	C
↗		H				
	→					I
	N		↑	E		

page 162

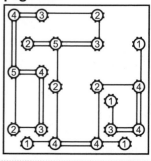